Theatre at work

Jim Hiley

Theatre at work

The story of the National Theatre's
production of Brecht's *Galileo*

Routledge & Kegan Paul
London, Boston and Henley

First published in 1981
by Routledge & Kegan Paul Ltd
39 Store Street,
London WC1E 7DD,
9 Park Street,
Boston, Mass. 02108, USA and
Broadway House,
Newtown Road,
Henley-on-Thames,
Oxon RG9 1EN
Photoset in 11/13pt Plantin by
Rowland Phototypesetting Ltd, Bury St Edmunds, Suffolk
Printed in Great Britain by
St Edmundsbury Press, Bury St Edmunds, Suffolk
© Jim Hiley 1981
Photography © Zoë Dominic

ISBN 0 7100 0815 5
ISBN 0 7100 0859 7 Pbk

For my mother

Contents

Acknowledgments

The number of people who ought to be thanked for their help with this book reaches three figures, and many of the names concerned occur in the text. In the circumstances, I hope they will forgive me if I confine myself to thanking Stephen Brook, John Russell Brown and John Goodwin for their help in setting up the venture; Martin Thurn for aid with research; John Dexter for obvious reasons; and Jon Ward, without whose practical help, professional advice and unending support the book's faults would have been many more than they are, and the author's state of mind infinitely more precarious.

Introduction

The dressing rooms at the National Theatre are on four floors, and built round a kind of quadrangle. Most of the actors can see and hear each other, as long as they are standing close to the windows. Stephen Moore and Michael Gambon, two of the longest-serving and most easy-going members of the National company, were especially given to exchanging banter across the courtyard. After the first performance of *Galileo*, Moore caught sight of Gambon, who had just given a three-hour exhibition of unexpected power in the title role of this difficult play. 'Well done, Gambon,' called out Stephen Moore. 'Well done, Mike,' added someone else. Actors are a much less demonstrative and self-congratulatory crowd than their image suggests. To-night, however, the forty-odd members of the cast gathered spontaneously at the windows and began applauding their leading man. It was their tribute to an unassuming actor who, by sheer dedication and without a hint of pretension, had inspired them through a tough rehearsal period. As the cheering grew, Gambon's dresser had to grapple with him to keep him at the window, and tears filled the actor's eyes. Nobody had witnessed such a scene at the National before. After a minute or so, Gambon shouted to the company to 'shut your row'; they laughed, and the ovation died down. Next morning – appropriately enough for an actor playing the visionary astronomer – Michael Gambon was hailed in the press as a new star.

With the odd exception, and well beyond expectations, the reviews were enthusiastic in praise of the production as well as its leading actor. This had been one of the National's biggest and costliest ventures, only its second original Brecht in almost two decades of putting on plays. The British theatregoer's customary antipathy to Brecht, and the fact that *Galileo* was staged at a time of diminishing prosperity for London's theatre, made it a sizeable gamble. Box office takings reinforced the critics' verdict that the gamble had paid off. Disaster had threatened more than once, however, and rarely was a triumph harder won.

John Dexter's production opened in the Olivier auditorium of the National Theatre on Wednesday 13 August 1980, after four unusually well-attended public previews. From before the start of rehearsals, I was given *carte blanche* to watch the work involved in getting *Galileo* on. I attended production meetings and rehearsals, and was allowed to roam unchaperoned the corridors, workshops and offices of the National probing what was happening or just soaking up the atmosphere. Photographer Zoë Dominic and her assistant Catherine Ashmore were given similar access, though they naturally visited the theatre less often than I. What follows – as best we can tell it – is the story of that production.

We wanted to find out how the National Theatre would tackle a vast play in its purpose-built, but still somewhat unfamiliar, new home. How was the initial idea for the show born? By what processes did that idea become performance? How closely did the end-product reflect the original aspirations? Who were the people concerned? How did they relate with each other and to what extent did they share a common cause? How was the National organised and what sort of place was it to work in? What sort of money was spent, and how carefully? What was the role of chance?

The story that attempts to answer such questions is primarily a story of effort – by carpenters, actors, welders, publicists, choristers, costumiers and a sprawling miscellany of working people. But the business of staging drama can be dramatic in itself. The process of producing *Galileo* involved as many peaks and troughs as the astronomer's career; sorrow succeeded elation which succeeded frustration; conspicuous success and fun for the many was accompanied by professional disappointment for the few. And there were 'big moments'. Little more than a week before rehearsals, for example, the show was nearly cancelled altogether, and a few days later one of the principal players astonished everyone by walking out. Comedy and tragedy against a background of slog: this is the reality of theatre at work.

Author's note

Prices, people's ages and other figures are given as in the summer of 1980, when *Galileo* was produced. Drawings used by kind permission of Jocelyn Herbert.

Chapter One

The National Theatre and the socialist classic

When Peter Hall took over as Director of the National Theatre in 1973, trouble engulfed him almost at once. The dream represented by the company's new home on the South Bank was rapidly turning into a nightmare. Completion of the building had been constantly delayed. The installation of its complex stage equipment hit repeated snags. Opening dates were announced, only to drift by without any opening taking place. In an attempt to force the pace, Hall led the National into its premises by the Thames without waiting for them to be finished. This should have been an administrative *coup*, similar to the transformation of the Royal Shakespeare Company's activities he had effected as its Director in the 1960s. But the theatre community was soon on the attack. Many of the critics joined in. The only riposte seemed to be the old formula of 'bums on seats'. Full houses might bring the security the National felt in desperate need of. A grand opening programme had already been slimmed down. Now, despite promises that it would not do so, the repertoire wore a conservative look.

The nature of subsidy restricted progress out of this mess. By comparison with others, the National's grant from the Arts Council of Great Britain is generous. To justify it, the theatre must offer a respectable programme while playing to large numbers of people. Poor attendances would be a scandal. On the other hand, it has been berated for purveying a 'safe' combination of popular classics and middlebrow new plays. The National must also earn an annual sum of a similar order to its grant. The familiar cry is that subsidised theatres experiment too extravagantly 'on the taxpayers' money'. The reality is the opposite. Luckier 'clients' of the Arts Council, such as the National, receive nearly but not quite as much as they need. To augment their grants with high box office returns, they are tempted to play safe. If their 'safe' offerings are successful, they are seen to be able to generate high income. This appears to justify the existing low level of subsidy. They then feel it necessary as well as desirable to experiment, in order to resume showing a loss. But they are in a vicious circle, and will soon be playing safe again.

The economic crisis that grew with the 1970s made matters worse for everyone. Then, in the spring of 1979, the National landed itself with a protracted spell of industrial action by back-stage staff. Many performances were given without the usual scenery, or were cancelled altogether. A former executive with the manufacturers of Kleenex, Michael Elliott, had just joined as administrative right-hand man to Hall. This reserved but steely mandarin was assigned to sort things out. After two acrimonious and confused months, said Elliott, 'we had virtually lost our audience.' In the wake of the strike, he admitted: 'We went for as popular a programme as possible.'

Throughout his period in charge, Hall had been wanting to stage *Galileo*. Under his predecessor, Lord Olivier, the National had put on Brecht's adaptation of Marlowe's *Edward II* and had imported directors from the Berliner Ensemble – the company Brecht founded – for a 'Brechtian' version of *Coriolanus*. Neither was a great success, and *Mother Courage* remained the sole original Brecht play attempted by Olivier. But Hall and his dramaturge, the enthusiastic academic John Russell Brown, believed the National should have done 'three or four' during its first quarter-century. At the outset of their regime, they opted for the accessible *Galileo*. Brown joked: 'It's more like other people's plays than the rest of the canon.' But the 1970s failed to provide circumstances in which Hall felt he could mount it, despite his assessment that *Galileo* and *Waiting for Godot* were 'the two big plays of the mid-century'.

Brecht's drama is set in seventeenth-century Italy. The leading character of the early scenes is a restless, pragmatic teacher of physics. He purloins a Dutch invention, the telescope, to earn much-needed cash. When he uses it to examine the skies, he soon finds evidence that the earth goes round the sun. So crucial is the idea that the sun revolves round a motionless earth to the philosophy of Church and State that Galileo's discoveries threaten the existing social order. He is at first patronised, and cajoled into silence. Then the ascent of a mathematician to the Papal throne encourages him to resume his dangerous researches, with a turbulent effect on the common folk. The new Pope is persuaded that the scientist should be threatened with torture by the Inquisition, and Galileo recants.

Whenever the National put *Galileo* into production, Hall and Brown knew they must get it exactly right. This would only happen in the teeth of professional and public resistance. The British theatre likes talk – witness the success of Shaw and Stoppard – but Brecht's ideas obtrude in a manner that is deemed vulgar. The dramatist's transgression is compounded by his intellectual concern for theatre itself. As a Marxist, he tried to evolve a theory and an 'epic' style of writing that would give dramatic form to dialectics and contribute to the betterment of the people's lot. Actors tend to go into rehearsals defying their director to turn them into 'Brechtian' artistes, and audiences into performances defying all concerned to show them a new kind of theatre they will prefer to the old. Prejudices have to be broken down whatever the subject-matter. This is not helped by Brecht's reputation among *cognoscenti* as a crucial figure in twentieth-century theatre.

Brecht completed his first version of the play in 1938, during his Scandinavian exile from the Nazis. The second he made in English with Charles Laughton toward the end of the Second World War. The bombing of Hiroshima was a major factor in their reshaping of the play, with its theme of the scientist's responsibility. By the time *Galileo* finally hauled itself on to the stage of the Olivier, its clear references to nuclear weaponry had a pointed topical reference in the debate about Cruise missiles. To avoid being attacked for propagandising, the National would need to offer a production that polished the play's theatrical virtues as brightly as possible. The delicacy of the position was demonstrated by comments Hall made on the afternoon of the official opening. On the one hand, he asserted that the play was nothing like as subversive as Brecht's disciples thought, and that it 'did the reverse' of making him want to be a Marxist. On the other hand, he said:

> 'It could be the mark of a mature society that it will pay to be criticised or challenged. I hope you will always see plays at the National that will upset *Time Out* [the radical London magazine] AND *the Daily Telegraph*.'

The first practical step toward its production of *Galileo* was for the theatre to obtain the rights – in the form of a 'licence' – to perform it. This proved no easy matter, and contributed, with a mountain of factors, to a feeling that the National's hopes were doomed. The Brecht estate is a notoriously jealous guardian of its principal's interests, and seldom keen to sacrifice potential royalties. On 13 February 1974, a marathon correspondence began.

Licences usually grant the National the right to perform a play for five years as long as it is given no less than thirty showings annually. In return, the management is guaranteed restrictions on productions by other theatres, especially in the London area. Officially, these 'territory' rights exist to protect the size of the theatre's potential audience; unofficially, they prevent simultaneous productions of the same play by major theatres, and the sometimes embarrassing comparisons that ensue. For *Galileo*, the National formally secured less rights than usual in this department. In practice, they were consulted over requests for the play from other theatres in this country and even in one case from Australia! Contrary to its reputation as a 'hoarder' of plays, the National agreed to more or less every request.

Most of the contention between the theatre's rights manager and the Brecht estate's English agents boiled down to money: how much would be paid to the estate for the planned stage performances, and how much in the event of the show being televised? Other arguments were over 'participation' – that is, what slice the National would take out of royalties on productions subsequent to its own. The theory behind 'participation' is that if the National has a success with a play, others will be encouraged to do it. As controversial as any other was the matter of translation.

At first the National had thought to use one of the several

existing English translations. In that case, said the estate, it must use either Desmond I. Vesey's or the Laughton version. Then Brown and Hall came up with the idea of having a new translation made. Hall felt Brecht had suffered from 'inept and fustian' translation in the past. He nurtured the hope that the National's *Galileo* would finally crack the British indifference to Brecht. This came to be shared by all who worked on the show, though they scarcely dared voice it until hours before the opening. So a translator was sought who would, in Brown's words, 'take on the whole imaginative job of making Brecht *there*.'

A young playwright of the Left had recently come within the horizons of the National's talent scouts. Hall said that, with the benefit of hindsight, it was 'obvious' he would be their choice.

After a redoubtable career on the 'fringe', notably with the Portable Theatre group, Howard Brenton had been given mainstream exposure when his play *Magnificence* was presented at the Royal Court in 1973. Brown and Hall saw it together, and liked it. One of their earliest joint commissions was a new play from Brenton. This was *Weapons of Happiness*, seen at the National in 1977, when it won an Evening Standard Drama Award. While *Weapons* was in production, they asked Brenton if he would be interested in translating *Galileo*. He agreed readily, but further difficulties ensued.

The estate has total power over translations: even a version made for private purposes can be seen as an infringement of copyright. John Coleby – the National's rights manager at the time – recalled that the estate was at first hesitant about the National's nominee. Coleby thought this was because Brenton had no 'track record' as a translator. Eventually, the estate agreed to his producing an edition. That did not, of course, guarantee permission to perform it, however much the National might be in favour. In addition, the translator's rights would be assigned to the estate. All royalties would be paid to the estate, who would in turn make part payment to Brenton. This was standard practice, but one which Coleby and others had been fighting to change. Since the new translation might never be staged, there would not necessarily be royalties anyway. Nevertheless, Brenton signed up to translate *Galileo* on 22 September 1977, and delivered at the end of the year. The National liked his version, and the Brecht estate wrote confirming its approval on 23 February 1978. But no licence had as yet been issued. Eighteen months later, the English agents and the theatre thought they had agreed on a mutually acceptable contract. This was sent to Brecht's son, Stefan, in the USA, and returned with a series of handwritten notes which considerably worsened the deal from the National's point of view. When the play finally opened in the summer of 1980, an advance on royalties had been paid by the theatre, but the elusive licence had still not materialised.

In appearance, Howard Brenton – a long, gangling man invariably dressed in denim – conforms to the hoarier image of revolutionary playwrights. But his manner is gentle to the point of bashfulness, and his commitment expressed with unwavering sobriety. Despite the uncertainties, translating *Galileo* was for him a labour of love. He considered it 'the great post-war play' and precisely the kind of 'socialist classic' the National was obliged to give voice to. He was in no doubt that the science pioneered and then betrayed by Galileo was a metaphor for contemporary Marxism. 'Against the notion that ideas don't have flesh and blood, it's about how ideas *are* flesh and blood.' As a Marxist himself, he had decided at the time of *Magnificence* that he did not want to be part of an 'alternative' culture. 'You should try to dominate the culture that exists, and invent furiously. You have to live with contradictions in the West. You should sharpen those contradictions, until They break, or chuck you out.'

Although it likes to think this does not affect its programming, the National – with Her Majesty the Queen as its Patron, and all three of its auditoria named after peers – is an outpost of Britain's establishment. But a relationship of uncanny harmony had developed between the theatre and Brenton, based on a kind of mutual usefulness. John Russell Brown felt strongly that Brenton was the person they needed for *Galileo*: 'We were looking for a certain kind of dramatist, who would respond to Brecht's concise yet open style, who was used to pitching scene against scene and voice against voice.' He had also been anxious about the long speeches in the last third of the play. He wanted a translator who would treat them, not as speeches with a capital 'S', but as 'real theatrical acts'.

Howard Brenton spent only six weeks at his task. He obtained from an academic he knew a literal translation of the play in German syntax, and read each of the existing English versions. Then he spent some time simply staring at the German text, and set out to include 'every verb, every image, every metaphor' in his own edition. 'By some luck,' he said, 'I produced a very accurate translation. It was like water divining. I hit a rhythm which is apparently very Brechtian.'

The estate found fault with only three phrases, specimens of what the dramatist admitted were 'unjustifiable licence'. In the scene of Galileo's recantation, for example, his pupil Andrea – referring abusively to the scientist's great appetite – calls him a 'snail eater'. Brenton replaced this with 'shit eater'; the estate objected, and 'snail eater' was restored.

As Brenton worked, he found himself drawn into an extraordinarily complex relationship between Brecht's language and English.

'Brecht admired English writing. We have an informal tradition which he was trying to inject into his own German text. The result is great formal language with a dirty underbelly. All the notes of cynicism, all the ironies come out in a very un-Schiller-like German.'

The underbelly was achieved less by slang than by anachronism. Throughout rehearsals, Brenton listened closely to the appropriateness of his own anachronisms, and made at least a dozen small alterations.

Brecht set out, according to Brenton, 'almost to rip off English theatre'. Much of his famous theory of 'alienation' was an attempt to get classical German actors to behave like their English counterparts. 'He was telling them to swan on and behave obliquely and rest back on the text. English actors don't realise they're half way there with Brecht because of our tradition of irony.' This sentiment was later echoed by both Hall and John Dexter; and Brenton noted approvingly that Dexter, rather than expounding wadges of theory, translated Brechtian attitudes into terms current among members of the cast.

Brenton's version was published as a National Theatre paperback. As things turned out, people buying it were slightly mistaken if they thought they had the text being given on the stage of the Olivier.

Shortly before the opening, the young dramatist said: 'This production is a test case, a test of what the English theatre should be doing. If they can't pull it off, the management should hang themselves from Waterloo Bridge!'

The problems with the Brecht estate, the industrial dispute and the move to the South Bank were by no means the only causes of *Galileo*'s postponement. After Brenton's translation arrived, a controversy blew up as to which of the National's main auditoria, the Olivier or the Lyttelton, the play should be staged in. The smaller Lyttelton, with its traditional pro-scenium arch design, was perhaps the more obvious choice. Brecht had kicked against the conventional theatre of his time, but the alternative techniques he proposed – a half-curtain, for example, to conceal scene-changes without pretending they were not taking place – were envisaged for the existing build-ings. In Brecht's time, as in our own, these were preponder-antly proscenium arch theatres. More practically, the swift changes of location in *Galileo* might be less easy to effect on the Olivier's open stage, given that most of its highly mechanised scene-shifting equipment was still not functioning properly.

Against these arguments, Brenton believed that the play was such a central piece of work that it ought to be done on the National's biggest platform. Hall, too, came to feel that this would be more appropriate. Brecht makes a great deal of how Galileo's discoveries undermined the distinction between earth and the heavens. They threatened the divisions between the people and their superiors, and presaged a new hegemony. Echoing this, Hall said: 'What I like about the Olivier is its feeling of a universe. On the best evening, the audience and actors really do become one.'

The public might have seen *Galileo* earlier had it been staged in the Lyttelton. The fact that it wasn't offers an intriguing comment on the National's architecture, as well as on the way its programme is planned.

The architect, Sir Denys Lasdun, had never previously built a theatre, but a panel of advisors – the Building Committee – met monthly to consult with him as he worked on the new National. Lord Olivier and Hall had been on this committee, alongside other superstars of the legitimate theatre. One of that group's crucial decisions was that the principal auditorium should be based on what was exciting to them at the time of their meetings, in the 1960s. They would not try to anticipate what would be in vogue in twenty years' time, nor be bound by the past. An arena, or open stage, was chosen, along a pattern not dissimilar to that evolved for the Royal Shakespeare's new Barbican theatre. But Olivier pointed out that many plays were written expressly with the proscenium in mind. It was hoped that major international companies would visit the new National: however would the Comédie Française manage, deprived of the familiar architecture? The solution was devastating in its simplicity, if not cheap. Two large theatres would be built, and the second would have a proscenium.

They were intended to be unidentical twins, architectural suitability alone determining which plays would go in which auditorium. But in the four or five years after the building opened, the more innovatory, problematical Olivier acquired a prestige – perhaps rooted partly in snobbery – that is not shared by the Lyttelton. There were puzzles, such as the transfer of Noel Coward's *Blithe Spirit* – a proscenium arch play if ever there was one – from the Lyttelton to the Olivier. And people at the National wondered why the New Year 1981 production of Shaw's *Man and Superman* was scheduled for the open stage. Hall insisted that 'large, resonant, universal theatre ought to be in the Olivier.' But the repercussions of this choice for *Galileo* were sometimes to prove vexing. Among them, economics reared its head again.

With over a thousand seats, the Olivier is a difficult auditorium to fill. Only about one-third of the playhouses in the 'commercial' West End have a similarly large capacity, and many of these were only half full at the time *Galileo* went on. The National relies in its budgeting on playing to at least eighty per cent capacity in the Olivier and the Lyttelton and seventy per cent in the Cottesloe studio. In the case of the Olivier, there is the further complication – acknowledged by National personnel – that they have not yet fully got the measure of the auditorium. As it happened, *Galileo* went a long way toward changing things, but this could not be guaranteed in advance. The economic crisis had already forced the National to drop two new shows per annum in each of its theatres. A production for the Olivier had become a frighteningly complex business. Hall said:

> 'We ought to do large scale European classics. Michael Billington and John Barber [theatre critics of the *Guardian* and the *Daily Telegraph* respectively] think we should do them all the time, but we can only do about one a year. We have already pulled off *Tales From The Vienna Woods* and *Undiscovered Country* in successive years and that's not bad.'

Galileo might not look like a risk, he added, but in the Olivier it certainly was.

While the Brecht play waited for a slot in the controversial auditorium, soundings began as to who might direct it and who take the lead. Finding the right combination took a year-and-a-half. His instinct told Hall he was the wrong person to direct. 'God knows I admire Brecht,' he explained, 'but I'm not sure I'm competent to direct him. I saw the Berliner Ensemble in the 1950s and they were so breathtaking it incapacitated me.' Alternative directors who might solve the problems of mounting the play on the Olivier's open stage were hardly profuse. Logistical competence is a much rarer quality among directors – including some who make a very nice living – than many playgoers would suspect. As for the actor, someone was needed who had bottomless vigour, maturity, enough 'star quality' to sustain a bravura performance over a long evening, and the nerve not to be put off by the character's prominent flaws. In addition, the actor and the director had to be acceptable to each other, as well as to Howard Brenton. Brenton rejected the names of a couple of directors, and a remarkable succession of pairings were proposed without coming to fruition.

By far the most popular choice as leading actor was Colin Blakely, the roly-poly performer with muscle underneath. But it is not easy to persuade artistes of his stature to take on a commitment involving a few performances over a long and possibly indefinite period, especially when – as was the case here – the role offers less secure rewards than those of, say, a Shakespearean hero. The names of William Gaskill and dramatist David Hare – who had directed *Weapons of Happiness* – were both linked with Blakely's. Apart from him, the only

'The Colin
Blakely of
tomorrow':
Michael
Gambon at an
early rehearsal
for *Galileo*

other suitable candidate in Brenton's mind was Albert Finney, who nearly did it with Lindsay Anderson directing. It is significant, as will become clearer, how many of these unsuccessfully mooted names have a past connection with the Royal Court Theatre.

With the possibility of Blakely receding, David Hare suggested that he might direct Anthony Hopkins in the title role. This was already more than a year after Brenton had submitted his script. Again, the deal failed to come off. Eventually, during one of the twice-weekly meetings of the National's top brass, Hall announced that he thought Michael Gambon should play Galileo.

It was an audacious suggestion. Gambon was an actor of unquestioned talent, who was then enjoying some personal success at the Lyttelton in Pinter's *Betrayal*. But his image was that of a middle-weight actor, with an aptitude for suburban men in the Alan Ayckbourn style. The most famous English-speaking incarnation of Galileo had been Charles Laughton: if Gambon was to follow in his footsteps, he would need to act in a way he had not been seen acting before. But Hall enjoyed the element of his job that made him an impresario. He was proud to have 'presided' over turning-points in the careers of now famous artistes: Vanessa Redgrave's performance as Rosalind and Peter O'Toole's Shylock were examples he would quote. Perhaps Gambon was approaching a turning-point. If they could not have Colin Blakely, Hall had decided, they would go for 'the Colin Blakely of tomorrow'.

On 14 July 1979, Hall reported back that he had spoken to Gambon and the actor had said yes. But a director had still not been found. Whoever took on the job now would have to accept that the most important piece of casting had already been done. The answer to their problems – and the cause of some future ones – was at hand. In fact, he was frantically busy rehearsing *As You Like It* for an August opening in the Olivier. After an absence of some years, a figure of almost legendary proportions had returned to the National. John Dexter was back.

Chapter Two

A *bijou* master

When the American comic actor Zero Mostel died, the grief of his erstwhile colleague John Dexter was mingled with indignation. At least, that's how Dexter's friend and preferred lighting designer Andy Phillips recalls it. Having worked with Mostel on the New York production of Arnold Wesker's *The Merchant*, they had both spent some time attempting to interest him in Brecht's anti-hero Galileo. They were beginning to be successful when Mostel died. This put paid to a pet project of Dexter's, and he could not conceal his exasperation.

Every globe-trotting director like John Dexter carries a portfolio of ventures he is keen to pursue, most of which never see the light of day. For years it looked as if Dexter's enthusiasm for *Galileo* was bound to be frustrated. He had seen the play first in 1957, and decided on the spot that he wanted to direct it. With others then working at the Royal Court Theatre, he had travelled purposely to see the Berliner Ensemble in Brecht's third and final version of the play, when it visited Paris. The young director was 'knocked out by it', and it is not hard to understand why.

John Dexter was at the heart of the great explosion that followed *Look Back In Anger* in the mid-1950s, when the British theatre acquired a social conscience. He was even talked of as something of a 'Brechtian'. The son of a plumber, he specialised in putting on the stage – particularly through the plays of Arnold Wesker – working-class people, such as the catering staff in *The Kitchen* and the national servicemen of *Chips With Everything*, who had tended in the past to appear only as supernumerary caricatures. With designer Jocelyn Herbert, he pioneered devices that have since become commonplace: leaving visible the real, bare walls of the stage, for example, and using metals and polystyrene in scenery rather than the prettier materials popular at the time. Dexter was also regarded as capable of staging the unstageable, a reputation reinforced later by his portrayal of horse-worship in *Equus* and Aztec rituals in *The Royal Hunt of the Sun*.

When Laurence Olivier started the National Theatre at the Old Vic in the early 1960s, Dexter left the Court to join the great man. With dramaturge Kenneth Tynan, he twice urged Olivier to tackle *Galileo* but to no avail. Peter Hall's arrival was potentially explosive. It was an open secret that Olivier had not been keen on Hall's succeeding him, but had favoured a group directorship which would have included Dexter. The latter's subsequent departure for New York undoubtedly prevented clashes with Hall, their both being strong-minded individuals. It was also part of a diminution of the Royal Court influence that had been formative to Olivier's regime. Dexter became Director of Productions at the Metropolitan Opera, and was no closer to staging his beloved *Galileo* until his collaboration with Zero Mostel.

In the summer of 1979, Dexter was still attached to the Met. He had not enjoyed a really big hit on the London stage since *Equus* six years earlier, and *Galileo* remained a fantasy. His return to the National was supposed to have been for work on a new play about Mozart and Salieri by Peter Shaffer, author of *Equus* and *The Royal Hunt of the Sun*. On this occasion, however, the director and dramatist clashed profoundly and parted company. Hall then asked Dexter if he had another project up his sleeve, mentioning that a Shakespeare would come in handy. Dexter had long wanted to do *As You Like It*, and had been the originally scheduled director of the National's all-male version ten years previously. Hall accepted the suggestion, but Dexter ended up with only four weeks for rehearsals. He had a hectic timetable organised so that he need not take lunch breaks but the actors would get theirs. Despite this, the reviews were disappointing.

Shortly before the critics pounced, on 28 July 1979 to be precise, Hall offered Dexter the Brenton translation of *Galileo*. True to the cliché, Dexter was in the bath when a way of making the play work in the Olivier came to him. On 9 August he told Hall he would do it. Inviting Dexter to direct the play

John Dexter and Michael Gambon at the first rehearsal of *Galileo*. (Behind them, wearing spectacles, is actor Michael Beint)

had not been an easy choice for Hall. Nevertheless, as the two men talked, the beginnings of a *rapprochement* between them occurred. A programme of work evolved, to execute which Dexter would continue to visit the National. It was to begin in the spring of 1980 with Sir John Gielgud playing Lear in the Cottesloe, and that would be followed immediately by *Galileo*.

Meanwhile, Hall had taken over as director of the new Shaffer. To rub salt in Dexter's wounds, *Amadeus* went on to become one of the company's biggest ever successes, with rewarding spin-offs such as a production on Broadway. When later Dexter felt he was not getting all the technical help he needed on *Galileo*, he would suggest, with some acerbity, that if this had been *Amadeus*, things might have been better.

Further complicating the relationship between Dexter and Hall was the fact that, as Director of Productions at the Met, Dexter was in a position to offer Hall work producing opera, which Hall relished. During the troubled year leading to *Galileo*'s arrival in the Olivier, the two men were actively negotiating for Hall to stage opera at the Met. Put crudely, each related with the other as both boss and employee. But as big a factor as any when Dexter was being considered for *Galileo* – and on the unfortunately large number of occasions after he had taken the job when the National considered dropping the production – was his personality.

In the theatre, there is a phenomenon known as the 'difficult' person, someone who manifests uncooperative and temperamental behaviour for reasons unfathomable to the 'well-adjusted'. Reputations for being 'difficult' are acquired with alarming ease, and John Dexter acquired one some time ago. His row with Olivier during their work together on *Othello* is one of the most celebrated in theatre history, and, among a bunch of apocryphal stories, it is even said that Dexter once *bit* an actor during rehearsals. Some people at the National felt he had 'homed in' on a couple of the younger actors in *As You Like It* with unreasonable persistence, and it was a fact that he had had another actor removed from the cast.

Michael Elliott said: 'John is difficult and spiky and sparky, and there's a reaction to an outside director coming in and upsetting people.' Dexter also inspires devotion, but a visiting director with devoted followers can be uncomfortable for a theatre. When Dexter and Andy Phillips – who had worked together on *As You Like It* – eventually outlined their production plans for *Galileo*, the Olivier's resident lights boffin said his reaction was: 'Oh fuck, they're here again!'

But the far from foolish Dexter had often rushed in where more angelic directors feared to tread. Consequently, he had brought off some of the most memorable examples of *mise-en-scène* in post-war theatre history. The National under Hall had never been so over-endowed with directing talent that it could now lightly ditch Dexter. With fifteen scenes spanning twenty-eight years, and over fifty characters not counting 'extras', *Galileo* is indeed an epic. It would make a tough proposition for any director, but was the kind Dexter appeared to thrive on. In addition, many actors positively revelled in his hard-driving approach. Selina Cadell, who played Audrey in *As You Like It* and Galileo's daughter, said:

> 'We all joke about the way he won't allow smoking and newspapers in the rehearsal room, but it's very good. It's tempting to get cosy and secure at the National. But Dexter cracks a whip and gets a lot of work done. Too many directors are satisfied too soon. If he's really cruel to someone, it's because he wants to kick their tricks away and get to the talent, to the truth.'

What was wrong with Dexter, she added, was his manner. 'He's probably the most vulnerable man in the building, but he should accept that actors are vulnerable like him.'

Another young admirer was Simon Callow, to whom Dexter gave his 'big break' as Orlando. He valued the way Dexter arrived at rehearsals with a very clear idea of how a scene should work – again, not something for which every director can be relied upon. 'He comes with it all ready and gives it to you,' said Callow. 'He doesn't tell you what the scene's about, but has a marvellous sense of when the baton passes from one actor to another. Peter Hall is prepared for the actor to take almost complete responsibility for his performance, but John sorts out all the problems.'

John Dexter is a small, round man with a faintly Oriental face – a sort of mandarin egg. He bristles with energy, and on occasion gives off an air of belligerence as if he were grappling with an invisible adversary. Equally often, and sometimes simultaneously, he generates devastating charm. That fruity-voiced, aristocratic actor Basil Henson once sat in the canteen at the National and announced that he had agreed to play the Pope in *Galileo* because he wanted to 'have a look' at Dexter. 'There is no doubt,' said Henson, 'that he is a master.' The actor drew on his cigarette and added: 'A *bijou* master.'

A remarkable number of aspirations collected around *Galileo*. Dexter had been attached to the play for over two decades. For nearly half that time, the National had been striving to put together its own production. Michael Gambon, now approaching middle age, had waited years for the kind of opportunity that was presenting itself and knew it would not beckon twice. Whether the actor's Ayckbournian image could be expunged, along with British audiences' resistance to Brecht and the memory of the failure of *As You Like It*; whether the *bijou* master could conjure up again the glory of his earlier career; and whether their corporate ambition for 'the great post-war play' could be fulfilled, remained to be seen.

Dexter and Gambon had last been together at the National in the Old Vic days, when the actor was playing the kind of role so small you miss it if you sneeze at the wrong moment. This might have made for tension, but the two met during the run of *As You Like It* and got along famously. Dexter later said that, if Gambon had not come as part of the deal, he would have asked for him anyway. Before returning to New York, he talked briefly with Gillian Diamond, the National's casting director, about the remainder of the company. Her title is a misnomer in the sense that Diamond's job is to help, not supervise, while a director recruits his players. But she has a simultaneous responsibility for developing the National's ensemble along lines agreed between her and Hall. Visiting directors sometimes get suspicious that actors are being suggested for purposes of the theatre's apart from the good of the production in hand. Discussions on *Galileo* weren't helped by the necessity of conducting most of them across the Atlantic.

The devotion Dexter inspires is reciprocated by tremendous loyalty. He likes familiar faces around, and takes particular

Simon Callow, whose ringing, actorly laugh was a much-loved –
and much-imitated – sound in the corridors of the National

pleasure in 'promoting' artistes he feels have shown promise. A young actor called Elliott Cooper was thus plucked from supernumerary status in *As You Like It* and awarded the part of Lodovico, the high-born fiancé to Galileo's daughter. Gillian Diamond said: 'Elliott was almost cast quicker than Gambon!' A clutch of other actors from the Shakespeare were pencilled in, including Simon Callow. As for the rest, on 16 August 1979 Dexter sent Diamond his preliminary ideas in a letter from the Met that read like 'Who's Who In The Theatre'. Sir Ralph Richardson was given as a possible Pope, and the distinguished actress Patience Collier as an Old Woman who speaks about half a dozen times. Collier didn't materialise, and the short scene concerned was cut anyway. Dexter had not wanted, he said, to be 'fobbed off' with inadequate casting.

Diamond's office subsequently drew up a suggested deployment of the National's smaller fry for the many monks, scholars and astronomers who impede Galileo's progress, but Dexter – barely recognising a name on the list – rejected it. Actors who thought they had been awarded parts were told they would now have to wait until the director's return to London, when these roles would be reallocated. Since Dexter's arrival was to be chronically delayed, this hardly diminished his reputation as a scourge of bit-part players.

During the autumn, Dermot Crowley was being discussed for the important role of Andrea, Galileo's most devoted pupil. As weeks went by, however, the luminous figure of Peter Firth came into view. In his teens Firth had made a huge impact as the boy who blinds horses in *Equus*, creating the role and playing it in London, Broadway and on film. As the play's director, Dexter had, people at the National would say, 'made' Peter Firth. It is certainly the case that Firth proceeded to a successful career after *Equus*, but never quite repeated its impact. Dexter had for a long time wanted to get the actor back into the 'straight' theatre, and had even tried to line him up as the Fool in *King Lear*, to play opposite Richard Burton. The culmination of Dexter's projected schedule with the National was to be Shakespeare's *Henry IV*, and he was determined that Firth should play Hal. But he felt the actor needed time to build up to such a part, particularly to develop his voice for the demanding auditoria of the National Theatre. A second programme of work was hatched, this time for Firth, beginning with Andrea. Gillian Diamond remembers Dexter telling her: 'I won't do *Galileo* without Peter Firth.'

Chapter Three

One room

In the preparatory phases of a large theatre operation, design – rather than casting – is the practical activity that serves as a medium for exploring interpretations. Things might be different in the best of all possible worlds, or even in the event of a true, permanent theatre ensemble being created. Then the evolution of performances and design would happen simultaneously and collectively over a sustained period. But in the present reality, actors can only be available for a few weeks before a show opens, whereas the design scheme for that show – costumes and stage furnishings as well as scenery – must be determined months ahead. As an embodiment of the director's ideas, the design pre-empts the work of the actors. A scale model of the set, and sometimes costume drawings, are presented to the cast at their first rehearsal. The director must either persuade them to fit in with this scheme, or expect a disharmonious end-product.

Dexter's formative thinking on *Galileo* was shared with his old friend, the designer Jocelyn Herbert. Having come together at the Royal Court under the late George Devine, Dexter's mentor and with whom Herbert lived, they liked to collaborate at every opportunity. Herbert – who was to have designed the Finney–Anderson production – was working with Dexter on two projects for the Met when he invited her to join him on *Galileo*. They spent most of the autumn together in New York, and swapped initial ideas on the play when they could find time away from the operas. Andy Phillips was confirmed as lighting designer. He, too, was from the Court stable, but of a later generation. When Phillips joined, the theatre's then-director William Gaskill asked him to create a new, British 'Brechtian'

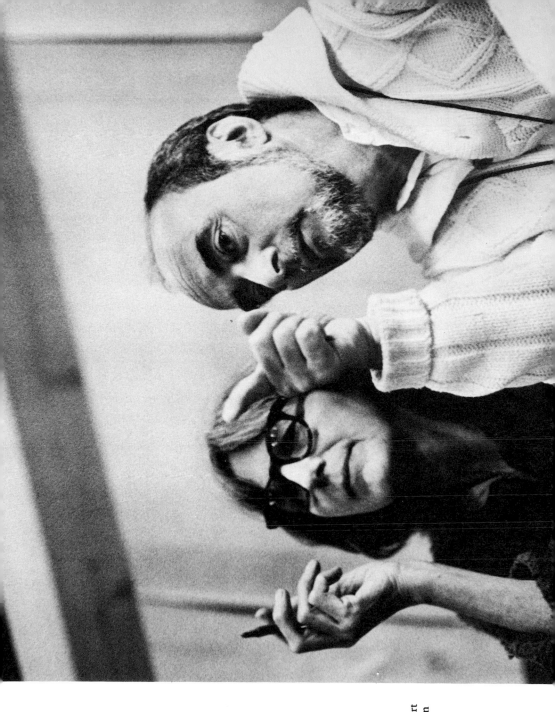

Designer
Jocelyn Herbert
(left) with John
Dexter at the
first rehearsal

style of lighting, which he went about in the process of lighting eighty consecutive shows at the Court over seven years.

They were an idiosyncratic trio, in the theatre's best traditions: Andy Phillips – stocky, bluff and singleminded; Jocelyn Herbert – a willowy woman whose Oxford English accent and remote manner veiled a passionate commitment; and Dexter, the man the other two loved to work for and occasionally loved to hate. All three shared a very pure philosophy about how things should look in a theatre. Herbert said:

> 'What interests me is to put as little, not as much, as possible on a stage, to evoke a period rather than represent reality. If you need a chair, and the play is set in a particular period, you try to have just one chair, beautifully made, that truly represents that period.'

Similarly, Phillips saw his task as to illuminate the space in which the play was to take place, without any 'tricks' or lighting effects that might come between the actor and the audience. Ideally, he said, a play's action would be lit by the same, single 'lamp' – the sun! His stock in trade was the lighting 'rig', a metal framework directly above the playing area from which the lights in use were unapologetically suspended.

If such ideas are familiar, they have become so during the working lives of these three musketeers against decoration, and no small thanks to them. The contrary pursuit of illusion remains strong, whether it be naturalist illusion, or *trompes d'oeil* in darkened theatres. Dexter and friends knew that this was partly the case at the National. Other factors, personal and professional, made their relationship with the South Bank venture and its emergent tradition even more charged.

Despite having been conspicuous for the most part by their absence, they felt an umbilical tie with the place. Dexter and Herbert had served on the Building Committee. A lot of what Lasdun had done, they liked. The architect had an especial regard for Jocelyn Herbert. Lasdun and she shared a disinclination to disguise materials: just as the set for *Galileo* was to include a profusion of timber and bare metal, so the concrete that holds up the National Theatre appears unadorned by plaster or paper throughout the auditoria and foyers. More eagerly, they concurred in mistrusting the stratified arrangement of proscenium arch theatres, preferring something more 'democratic'.

A turning-point in the committee's deliberations was reached when Lasdun sketched a simple square, representing the projected Olivier theatre, with one corner marked out as the stage. This suggested a single room in which actors and audience would come together, rather as they do at the Chichester Festival Theatre where the National company began in embryo. This was the committee's 'Scheme B'. What was eventually built, however, was 'Scheme E'.

Lasdun believes the existing auditorium reflects the 'all-in-together' principles of 'Scheme B', but Dexter and others are not so sure. For them, the acting area recedes too far, edging back into a room beyond that in which the audience are sitting. Encased by the backstage areas and the 'fly tower' above it, the stage has what Dexter called 'the widest proscenium arch in the world'. This and the height of the circle make intimacy between actor and audience – a strong feature at Chichester – difficult to achieve. Director and designer face the problems of a conventional theatre without its advantages: an early scheme for *Galileo* involved a half-curtain but this was quickly dropped.

The rationale for the elaborations on 'Scheme B' revolved partly round scenery. In the proscenium arch design, there is 'wing' space at the side of the stage from and to which settings can be shifted. In addition, there is usually a fly tower above, from which can be lowered flat screens of scenery, curtains, and other two-dimensional pieces to add to the effect. But the Olivier is intended to be an 'arena' stage and was built without wings. Its fly tower was designed to store scenery that would normally go in the wings as well as to serve its own more traditional functions. Because of the need to contain three-dimensional lumps of scenery, a unique system of mechanised 'flying' was employed in addition to the usual pulleys. This is supposed to co-ordinate electronically with a drum-shaped elevator below the stage, which in turn is designed to raise complementary pieces of scenery into the view of the audience. Unfortunately, neither the 'power flying' nor the 'drum revolve' have ever functioned to the satisfaction of National personnel. Indeed, the drum revolve must be one of the most famous pieces of stage machinery never to have been seen by paying customers!

Purists point to Chichester and pooh-pooh the need for

quantities of scenery. The fact has to be faced, however, that the Olivier is the principal auditorium of the National Theatre of Great Britain. Wouldn't we feel cheated if we couldn't see a little spectacle there once in a while? Certainly, it must have been hard for the seasoned professionals on the Building Committee to resist retaining at least the possibility of a little lavish décor.

Dexter's people reviled the fly tower, in particular, and the drum revolve. Dexter said he always argued against both on the Building Committee and neither he nor Herbert could remember that group agreeing to their inclusion. But Herbert pointed out that even the purest-minded director can't resist the fly tower now that it exists. Dexter announced at the outset that he wanted to do *Galileo* on as bare a stage as possible, but would occasionally – if wistfully – suggest adding pieces by means of flying.

Hall and Lasdun said that a fly tower of some kind was always planned, and Lasdun has verbatim transcripts of the Committee's proceedings. (He intends to have these released only after his death.) But there is no doubt that the drum revolve was introduced after the Committee's deliberations, on the advice of a firm of consultants about whom National staff now mutter darkly and often.

The firm was Theatre Projects Consultants Ltd and its chief Richard Pilbrow. He had been lighting director for the National Theatre, and, until he formed his consultancy, a member of the Building Committee. As a lighting designer, the world-renowned Pilbrow was regarded as the figurehead of an aesthetic approach by Andy Phillips and others, who prefer the hard white light of Brechtian tradition.

It is worth contemplating this network of relationships to understand some of the tensions that were to arise on *Galileo*. Pilbrow's company was identified with the National's flying facilities and other machinery of which Dexter and friends were suspicious. As a designer, he had a number of stalwart admirers among the resident lighting team at the Olivier with whom Phillips would need to collaborate. Bill Bundy, the National's technical administrator and keeper of its production purse, once worked for the Theatre Projects empire. Another of Pilbrow's associates was David Hersey; he was a regular lighting designer

for Peter Hall. As a final thread in this cat's-cradle of philos-
ophies and historical associations, Andy Phillips had been out
in the cold following his abrupt departure from one of the
National's earliest productions on the South Bank.

With some, if not all, of this in mind, Jocelyn Herbert had a
model of the Olivier stage made for her to work on during her
autumn sojourn in New York. At the director's suggestion,
Hayden Griffin's designs for *As You Like It* were taken as a
starting-point for *Galileo*. Griffin and Herbert thought alike,
and there was a proposal in the air that they should work jointly
on Dexter's forthcoming programme at the National. For this,
as for most of her projects, Herbert used a mass of sketches with
the model rather than detailed design plans. She and Dexter
passed endless little drawings to and fro as they talked. Dexter
would seek her ideas not just on how the set might look, but
also about how the action might move upon it. In their collaboration, the dividing line between design and 'blocking' was
always fluid; later, Herbert would watch rehearsals and offer
comments on the actors' moves, just as now Dexter was scribbling his own notions onto sketches she had made.

Very early on, the idea of a screen for slide projections was
born. This was to have two functions. Brecht recommended
slides to locate the action firmly in its historical context, and
to announce what was about to happen so that surprise would
not dislodge the audience from an attitude of scrutiny. For
Herbert's more immediate purposes, a large screen judiciously
placed might give the impression that the back of the Olivier
stage was not as far away from the spectators as in fact it was.
She hoped this would have the effect of keeping the action in
the 'same room' as the audience, and shutting off that part of the
stage that was behind the unintended proscenium. Her original
thought was to build a framework into which could be dropped
three-dimensional scenery, to give an occasional sense of perspective, as well as the projection screen. The former element
was later rejected, but the framework and screen remained.

A second important concept was that the acting area should be
built higher than the existing stage, and brought out towards
the audience. This was something many designers had done in
the Olivier – even those less wedded to the arena principle than
Herbert – and her first sketches used a rectangular platform like

Griffin's for *As You Like It*. But she was far from satisfied. For her, the corners of this stage jarred with the arcs of Lasdun's auditorium. And it was all very well for Dexter to go on about keeping the stage bare, but Brecht's script demanded a large amount of 'props' and furniture – how could these be moved smoothly on and off an area built so far forward?

By the time she left New York, she had broken her wrist and nothing had been decided upon. But at least Dexter agreed they were on the right lines. She returned to London with her head full of the Olivier, and got together to talk about it more with Hayden Griffin. Soon she decided that she wanted to design a whole new stage for the auditorium. It would be a permanent fixture, not just for *Galileo* or Dexter's season of plays. This was an extraordinary demonstration of her concern and dedication. Without being asked, she spent weeks hatching a plan. In February, intending no more than to open up a discussion, she showed her work so far to the National's high-ups and to Lasdun. Although the architect had reservations, she was surprised by the warmth of the reception. Suddenly the National was saying that it thought it should build the stage she had designed. A scheme evolved whereby the new stage would be incorporated into her designs for *Galileo*, and would be erected in the Olivier when the Brecht play set was installed.

What had happened was not as simple as a conversion to the Dexter–Herbert ideology on the part of the National. Hall had been worried for some time about the length of 'change-overs' between shows in the Olivier. By the time the set for one play had been taken down and replaced by that for the next play in the repertoire, there was little time left for rehearsals. There were other logistical problems. The Lyttelton had been built with an area at the back of the stage the same size as the stage itself. This 'rear stage' was for the storage of sets. In the Olivier, the 'rear stage' was much smaller than the stage proper for the simple reason that the fly tower and drum revolve were supposed to take scenery. Since they were not doing so as planned, and since so many sets comprised rostra to raise the height of the stage as well as conventional scenic pieces, a storage crisis was building up. Inspectors from the Greater London Council were looking askance at sets stacked up in backstage corridors. A single, new stage that would incorporate the designers'

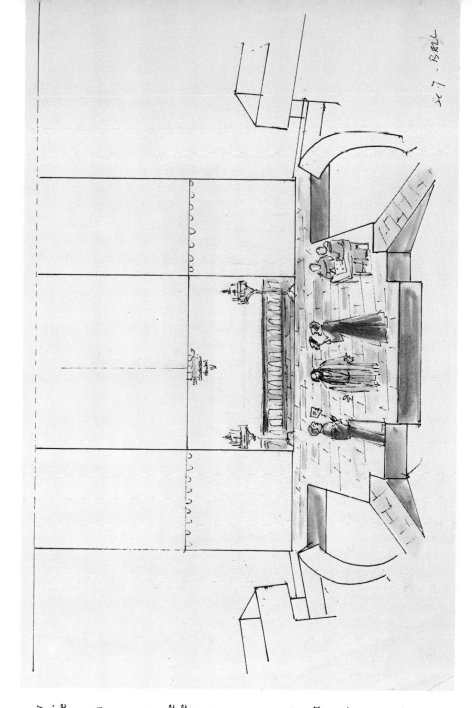

Figure 3.1 An early drawing by Jocelyn Herbert. At this stage, the rectangular shapes of the main acting area reflect Hayden Griffin's design for *As You Like It*. Slides would be projected on to a screen in the framework at the back. The scene illustrated takes place at a formal ball: the balustrade behind the actors was to cause much contention. The odd shapes to the left and right of the stage represent the extreme sides of the Olivier audience area, including the 'boxes' in which would sit the choir and the narrator or 'Speaker'

tendency to build 'up and forward' might simultaneously save space and create more time for rehearsals.

After Christmas, in short, things were looking good for Dexter's people. They were being welcomed back to the fold, and the prospects for *Galileo* were exciting if fluid. Then the first of the big disasters struck. Dexter – still in New York – became ill. He had never had an easy time at the Met. Now his troubles were compounded by a bout of painful and debilitating shingles. He was due back in London shortly to start *King Lear* with Gielgud but his illness looked as if it was going to be prolonged. Out of the blue, the National received a phone call from the veteran actor to say that he did not want to go ahead with this project after all. His decision had nothing to do with Dexter's health, but it mitigated the situation temporarily.

As the weeks went by, though, Dexter remained virtually incommunicado. Anxiety rose among those working on *Galileo*. It was impossible for Jocelyn Herbert to make progress with the design. Initial ideas are invariably followed by better ideas, she explained, but you can't pursue them if you can't share them with your principal collaborator.

She had begun to think in terms of a circular playing area in front of the screen, built above or marked out on the new stage. This disc would, she believed, complement the auditorium's architecture better than the sort of rectangle that had been employed on *As You Like It*. For the five or six scenes set in Galileo's houses, which she felt needed quantities of furniture as well as walls with doorways, she had come up with a 'truck' or moving platform. With the appropriate scenery laid out on it, the truck would travel from the rear stage up on to the disc and serve as the playing area for the scene concerned. Afterwards, it would travel back out of the audience's view, and could be rearranged for the next scene in which it was to be used.

Without Dexter's reactions, however, Herbert could make nothing of such notions. But the National continued to press her for details – in particular of how much the set was likely to cost – because its financial situation was worsening daily. The trouble was compounded by Mrs Thatcher and the spending cuts her new Conservative administration had brought with it. By April, the optimism that opened the year at the National had turned decidedly sour.

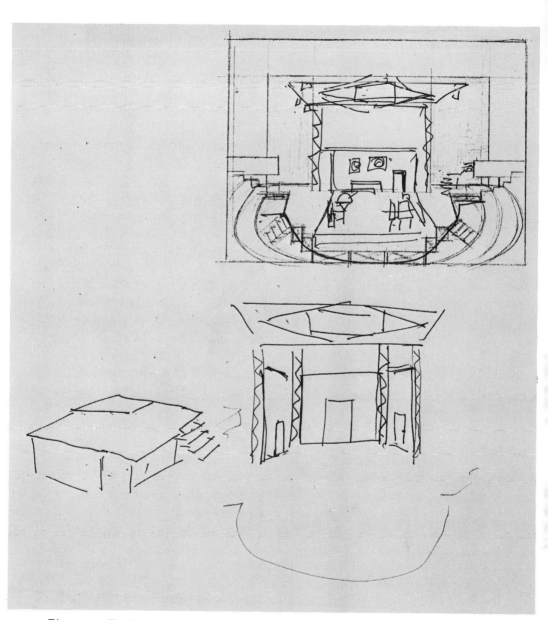

Figure 3.2   Design in action: many of Herbert's ideas were drawn
onto photocopied plans of the basic stage. Above she has sketched
in a more circular shape for the main acting area, and a lighting rig
above it. Below is one of her first drawings of the rear framework
with its sides angled toward the audience, contrasting with the flat
effect of her earlier ideas

Chapter Four

The best laid plans . . .

Mrs Thatcher had introduced reductions in spending for nearly every department of government. While Dexter was groaning with shingles in New York, the Arts Minister, Norman St John Stevas, was involved in a drawn-out struggle with his colleagues in Whitehall to keep the grant to the Arts Council at something like its existing minimal level.

A grotesque ritual occurs annually at the end of winter: the Arts Council is kept waiting to hear how much it will be allocated in the rapidly approaching financial year, then the Council keeps its clients in suspense while sorting out how to divide up its funds.* This last-minute agony makes planning – the prerequisite of good housekeeping in any activity – impossible, with a damaging side-effect on the artistic community's morale. But in 1980 the delay was made greater than ever by the new fanaticism for cuts. At the National the upshot was that it did not know until April what its grant would be for the financial year which began in that month. Not only did another round of economies have to be made, the management was also obliged to submit balanced budgets in detail such as had not previously been required before it could draw the cash.

Despite the vestige of bohemianism that clings to the image of theatre people, they need to be extremely well organised in this day and age. As Michael Elliott pointed out, manufacturers think in terms of a ninety-nine per cent failure rate on new consumer products, even after market testing. A theatre can't research in advance the response to new productions, but a single failure can have drastic repercussions. The irony of the

* By contrast with its usual practice, the government announced its 1981–2 allocation of funds to the Arts Council in December 1980.

crisis now descending on the National was that, since joining, Elliott had tried strenuously to improve the theatre's planning and thence its housekeeping. Along came the Tories, alleged friends of the businesslike, and disrupted the planning process violently.

Elliott had never intended his new schemes to reduce flexibility, because he recognised that it was essential to the atmosphere surrounding artistic endeavour. He wanted decisions made in the same atmosphere, but earlier. Earlier decisions, especially about design, would enable the smoother movement of set building and so on through the National's workshops, and reduce the need for expensive contracting-out of work (not to mention overtime!). Although limited facilities sometimes make it unavoidable, the National sees contracting-out as a sign of failure. Its planning is, however, made even more complex by the fact that three theatres are housed under the same roof and served by the same workshops, and that the two largest theatres each operate a repertoire system with four or five shows rotating at any given time. Add productions in the planning stage to those in, entering or departing the repertoire and on tour, and the National is quite likely to be concerned with over a score of shows at the same time.

As technical administrator, Bill Bundy was in overall charge of the 'backstage' operation. When Michael Elliott arrived, he asked Bundy to jot down the problems besetting him. Bundy's paper suggested a formula, which Elliott then crystallised and put into practice at the end of 1979. This was for a 22-week schedule affecting plays in the Olivier and Lyttelton. No play could in future be decided upon less than 22 weeks before its first performance. For plays in the Olivier the main points in the cycle were as follows, working down from Week 22:

Week 22   play decided on
Week 20   director, designer and lighting designer chosen
Week 16   outline design for set and costumes proposed

The National's staff would then have a fortnight to discuss with designer and director the likely cost of what had been put forward, and to work out amongst themselves how the new show would fit in practically with others in the repertoire – how easy storage and change-overs would be, for example.

Week 14   final design arrived at; by now a model of the set
           would be built and budgets agreed on
Week 12   drawings of the set with measurements submitted
           by designer; from these, much more detailed
           drawings of each component job would be
           made for the benefit of the theatre's workshops
Week 10   making of set, props and costumes commences
Weeks 2   the now completed set installed in the rehearsal
  and 1   room for the use of actors and director
Week 0   Production Week

The production week began with the set being moved into the theatre – the process known as the 'fit up'. Technical and dress rehearsals would follow, and the week would usually climax with a first public preview on the Friday evening.

On *Galileo*, the first two stages had been accomplished well in advance of the deadlines. But Week 16 occurred early in April, when Dexter was still laid up and Herbert was adamantly refusing to commit herself to designs she had not had a chance to discuss with him. Unresolved questions included whether there would be screens for slide projections additional to the main one in its framework. Smaller screens upstage and down-stage of it, on either side of it, and at the extreme sides of the auditorium were possibilities Herbert mulled over with her young assistant Peter Hartwell. And there was the problem of the cavernous area behind the main screen. This was not going to be used much, but still some covering had to be decided on for the huge metal shutters that marked the back of the stage proper. Tradition suggested long black curtaining – 'drapes' – but, again, Herbert was unsure.

Things had remained superficially amicable. Meetings about the new stage continued. Herbert was busy on another National production, *Early Days*, which was to move to the Cottesloe after opening in Brighton at the end of March. But communication over *Galileo* inevitably became strained. The National's production office kept phoning up the designer, hoping for decisions, but only to hear possibilities. Confusion arose as to which was which. Particularly worrying to the National were the practicalities of the back-projections and the cost and manoeuvrability of the truck. Drawings had been sent over to

Bill Bundy, technical administrator, pictured during the
production week of *Galileo*

New York, but the theatre suspected Dexter's staff were keeping them from him owing to the delicacy of his health. Peter Hartwell recalled: 'The pressure from the National was very irritating, but we told ourselves it was better to get the decisions right. We were working to John Dexter's schedule rather than the National's.'

It was a classic formula for mistrust: the theatre had its own good reasons for wanting early answers, the design team had theirs for holding out. The opening date was put back by a week, and Dexter's health began to improve, but the situation remained fraught.

The lugubrious Bill Bundy was up to his eyes in budgets and being forced to delegate more work on *Galileo* than he would have liked. Every time he tried to assess the financial position with Michael Elliott, it appeared to have worsened. From what he could gather of the design plans, Bundy was discovering – as Herbert had before him – that Brecht built some of his plays on a larger model than Shakespeare. 'We were caught out by *Galileo*,' he admitted ruefully. 'It's more than an epic. It's bigger than Shakespeare.' For his part, Elliott had seen more shows come in under budget than not since the inauguration of the 22-week scheme, but the budget busters tended to be shows that fell behind schedule. *Galileo* was, of course, very behind. Of the designs, Elliott said: 'Every time we saw them they seemed to have gone up £5,000.'

On 10 April Mark Taylor, from the National's production office, visited Herbert's Holland Park studio and photographed her model of the set such as it was. Taylor then studied it with his chief, Bill Bundy, and the two of them went to see Herbert together a week later. Their message was simple: money was running out. After more to-ing and fro-ing between South Bank and studio, Herbert reluctantly agreed to fly out to see Dexter. The object of the trip was to arrive at some definite decisions, the cheaper to execute the better. On 24 April, Mark Taylor escorted the designer to the airport, carrying her model. As she left, he prayed that Dexter, the master *metteur-en-scène*, would be persuaded to cut the truck. The following week would be Week 14.

Dexter was still poorly, but the two friends spent a long weekend going through the play scene by scene. Walls, doors

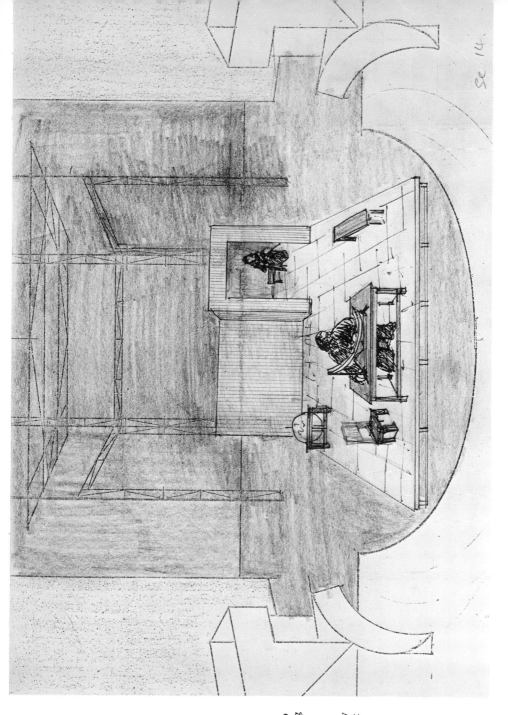

Figure 4.1
This version of
the truck –
which would
travel from
behind the
framework on to
the main playing
area – carries
scenery as well
as furniture.
Here the scenery
creates the effect
of an ante-room
to Galileo's
study for the
penultimate
scene of the
play. The
drawing also
shows how
skeletal the
framework has
become

Sc 14.

and some furniture were discarded. Dexter revealed that he was thinking of cutting a short sequence in which Galileo is seen to press on with his researches despite a widespread plague. This would do away with the exterior of two houses. They opted to use just the one main screen. This decision might have led to a reduction in the size of the framework, since it had been designed large enough to hold companion screens on either side. But Herbert liked the framework as it stood, and Dexter concurred. They decided not to employ drapes: the magnificent shutters at the back of the stage could stand unmasked. The truck was definitely 'in'. The National might not like all these decisions, but at least they had now been made.

Back in London, a big shock awaited Herbert. The new stage she had conceived, the theatre told her, could not now be built. This foundation of her design for *Galileo* was too expensive. The news made her question how sincere the National's conversion to the idea had been in the first place. And why, she asked, had she been allowed to discuss designs with Dexter on a basis that no longer existed?

The new stage would have had to be installed over a weekend. This would have minimised performances lost, but made for heavy overtime payments. Its supporting substructure would have been complicated because the surface of the drum revolve could bear less weight than the rest of the existing stage. And redesign and some re-rehearsal would have been necessary for productions already in the repertoire. Bill Bundy had totted up the cost, including loss of income, and arrived at a prohibitive figure of £80,000.

Having postponed the new stage to April 1981, the National then considered calling off the whole show. *Galileo* was already looking expensive, and could be relied upon to become more so. Paradoxically, individuals such as Bill Bundy who appeared obstructive to the *Galileo* team, were among those lobbying most vigorously to keep the production in the schedules. The National needed Dexter, they argued, and Dexter – after a protracted illness and the drubbing his efforts at the Met had received – probably needed the National.

Meanwhile, Herbert again found herself expected to produce new ideas without her director to consult. She suggested that the circular playing area alone could be built to the height

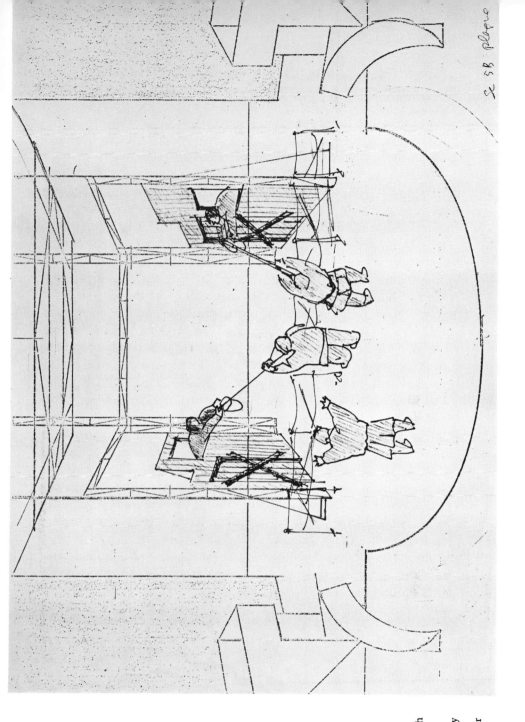

Figure 4.2
Sketch for the
'plague'
sequence. Both
the scene and
the idea of
placing scenery
in the frame-
work were later
dropped

originally proposed for the new stage, and cantilevered to look as if the disc was floating. The truck would be square. The juxtaposition of square and circle was important to Dexter and Herbert. It had an astronomical connotation, and it reflected the idea of the round stage in the corner of a square room which was how they thought of arena theatre.

In the middle of May, the National made what it thought – mistakenly – was the final decision to go ahead with *Galileo*. But Herbert was told that the disc could not come out as far toward the audience as she had hoped, and the metal shutters at the back of the stage could not be used. Part of the reason for this was that the central shutter would have to be raised each time the truck came forward and this would make a distracting noise. She suggested that the shutter could be permanently raised, and an imitation, soundless shutter built immediately behind it to let the truck through. This was not possible, she was told, because it would get in the way of the back-projector.

Bundy now estimated that it would cost £50,000 to get the show on stage – not counting internal labour – and he had found the last £8,000 of this by trimming the budgets of other productions. In the circumstances, the *Galileo* team's reaction to the good tidings was tinged with cynicism. Why couldn't this money have been found earlier? Might it have been found quicker if somebody else had been directing? They resented being held to ransom. This was rather how the National's production office now felt as they found themselves hammering on Herbert's door once more for design decisions. But she and Hartwell were busy incorporating the recent changes into their model to show Dexter when he arrived. On top of this, Hartwell had asked for time off to work on a show of his own at a stage when the future of *Galileo* looked bleak. Herbert had felt she couldn't refuse, but his absence would mean further delays to the preparation of drawings for the workshops.

At this point, the National took a calculated risk that might have proved very costly. The truck would require engineering the theatre felt its workshops were not equipped to carry out. P. E. Kemp Engineers Ltd, the firm it hoped to use, were accruing a packed order book, no small thanks to the forthcoming Drury Lane musical *Sweeney Todd*. To avoid being turned down later, the National commissioned Kemp's to construct the truck even though the finer details of it had not been approved by Dexter.

The director, meanwhile, might have been suffering from shingles but was unaffected by Mrs Thatcher's austerity. He would be arriving in England at the end of May, it was learned, on the *QE2*.

His disembarkation would coincide with Week 10.

Chapter Five

Heads down

Although he was due to start rehearsals in a fortnight's time, Dexter went straight from Southampton to Jocelyn Herbert's farmhouse in the country. Listening to music and drinking wine, they found the odd occasion to enjoy themselves. *Angst* enveloped them for the most part, however, as they worked on *Galileo*. Dexter complained about the latest pronouncements from the National. The management seemed to be denying him things that had been intended for the production since it was first discussed the previous summer. Flexibility at what was, after all, one of the world's newest theatres was in shorter supply than at the much older Met, or even than it had been at the Vic. He and Herbert proceeded to draw up the last concessions they were prepared to make on the set, and to discuss matters like costume which had so far been perilously neglected.

Week 9, Tuesday

Dexter and Herbert were at the National for a production meeting. This was to be the first glimpse of Dexter for many of the theatre's backstage captains, and the occasion for him to present his final compromises. Beforehand, he talked grimly. It would be 'heads down for a pitched battle', and if he did not get his way he might have to talk ultimata with Hall. But that afternoon, as a dozen or so people crammed in a fourth-floor office among discarded models from long-forgotten productions, Dexter was all avuncularity and the mood was cautiously friendly. There was a stream of slightly aggressive jokes – 'Bill Bundy will like this,' Dexter kept saying – but at least they were jokes. He opened with a short architectural history, starting at Chichester and zipping through the life of the Building Committee to their present dilemmas. He and Herbert had spent the past year solving problems that would not have been problems in a proscenium arch theatre. 'We can't change the set any more,' said Dexter, 'we've changed it four times. We're running out of ideas.'

Herbert then talked the play through from first scene to last, while Peter Hartwell operated the model – as perfect and detailed as a Victorian toy theatre, with tiny replicas down to the last stick of furniture. There were no walls left in the truck scenes, and no 'perspective' pieces dropped in behind the screen framework. There was one big addition, however, a bombshell for most of those present. If they couldn't use the metal shutters, Dexter and Herbert wanted a pale-coloured surround right across the back of the stage, to replace black drapes and match the surface of the disc. Somebody later estimated this would cost £3,500. Throughout, the meeting was haunted by questions of money.

The atmosphere stiffened appreciably as the discussion moved to lighting. Yet another effort was made to get rid of the lighting rig. The objections were practical as well as aesthetic, but Phillips was pugnaciously cool and Dexter backed him to the hilt. The rig was integral to the design: they were not to be shifted.

Nobody could work out how to effect the back-projections, even given that the use of slides had been considerably reduced. In Phillips's usual hard white light, the projector would need to be super-powerful. A more vexing question was where it would be located. It could not be at the same level as the screen because the new surround would be in the way. Perhaps it should be higher than the surround and projecting down on to the screen at an angle? But the existing gantry high up at the back of the stage was overloaded with projection equipment for *Amadeus*. This revelation prompted Dexter to splutter that one show in the repertoire couldn't be allowed to jeopardise another. Bill Bundy knew of only one or two makes of projector in the world that could do the required job, and they cost about £5,000 each. With his cigarette in his mouth – a permanent fixture like Andy Capp's – Phillips screwed up his eyes and peered at the model. After a momentary pause he said: 'That's cheap.'

The surround, the back-projection and the rig were 'in'. Dexter was available to talk to 'upstairs' at any time. 'We'll have to go back to the drawing board,' said Bundy quietly as the meeting broke up, 'and do some more costing.'

Dexter may not have appreciated the significance of Bundy's remark at once, but he knew all about it on the following Friday evening. He was asked then to meet Hall and Elliott in Hall's office. Once again, the National were questioning the whole venture. The design scheme as presented at the production meeting, they told Dexter, was too expensive. For all publicity material had been printed, for all Gambon had been back at the National since the autumn, waiting for *Galileo* – for all, indeed, a book was now being written about the production – it could not go ahead as it stood.

Dexter eventually consented to further economies, and attention focused on the wardrobe. Herbert agreed that the large carnival crowd who appear rioting in excitement at Galileo's discoveries would be costumed from 'stock' – that is, they and certain other briefly seen characters would wear clothes from previous productions rather than be costumed specially. Enough agreement was reached for the ultimatum to be withdrawn, but matters such as the surround remained irritatingly unresolved.

Shortly before the encounter in Hall's office – the 'crunch meeting' Elliott called it – the start of rehearsals was put back by a week. When the opening had been postponed, the beginning of rehearsals remained as scheduled to allow leeway in case Dexter's illness recurred. Rehearsals were now reduced to their originally planned length, which nobody felt would be a problem as long as Dexter stayed healthy. It was, perhaps, pleasantly surprising that a relapse had not been brought on by the casting foul-ups which caused this latest delay.

In the words of Gillian Diamond's assistant, Ann Robinson, Dexter found the children she had recruited too 'classy'. Apart from three youngsters among a crowd in the final scene, and a daughter for the balladeer who entertains at the carnival, the play has two important roles for boys: the young Andrea, and Galileo's Florentine patron, Prince Cosimo de Medici. Robinson had a normally infallible system of sources depending on the social group of the character concerned. She would try to avoid stage schools – a little *passé* nowadays – but would go to the legendary Anna Scher's Children's Theatre in Islington for 'basic, rough' youngsters. (That means 'working class', but they don't use such expressions at the National Theatre!) On this occasion, Robinson had gone too up-market for Dexter's taste, and had made another mistake in casting children of the same age as the characters. For the Olivier, Dexter felt he needed slightly older boys.

This meant demotion for nine-year-old Stephen Rooney, whom Robinson had had in mind for the prince. When Timothy Norton was given this role by Dexter, Robinson suggested young Rooney understudy the part. The director upset her plan, however, by appointing an understudy from elsewhere in the cast. Rooney was distraught, being left with a small non-speaking role as one of the Pope's attendants. To compensate, Robinson later offered him the boy Jesus in *The Passion*, then being prepared for the Cottesloe. But Rooney was by that time enjoying *Galileo* so much that he declined promotion up the Christian hierarchy.

The most significant child in the play is the young Andrea, who has a number of demanding early scenes with Galileo. The actor recruited would need to resemble Peter Firth, who was to appear as his older self. Marc Brenner turned out to be one of Dexter's most inspired pieces of casting – as well as one of his staunchest disciples – but he landed this role only by an extraordinary coincidence.

There was very little theatre in Brenner's background. At the time of *Galileo* he had played only a couple of amateur roles and was rehearsing once a week for his local youth club play. On Thursday 29 May, he persuaded his father to take him along to an additional, one-off rehearsal at the club. For some reason the session was abandoned. While Brenner senior and junior were hanging around the foyer trying to find out what was happening, a call came through from a theatrical agent. She was looking for a dark, Jewish boy to play a concentration camp victim. Although Brenner is Jewish, he is neither dark nor of the undernourished mien that was required. On an impulse, however, his father put his name forward. Next morning, the agent told the boy at once that he was completely wrong for the camp victim. But by this time an emergency call from the National had reached her. Noticing the similarity of Brenner's fair features to Peter Firth's, she sent him along to meet Ann Robinson that same afternoon. All of a sudden, thirteen-year-old Brenner — who did not even want to be an actor when he grew up — was moving in theatrical London's most elevated circles. He 'read' for John Dexter on the day of the production meeting. On Wednesday 4 June, the agent phoned to say that he had got the part and should be ready to start on the following Monday.

The casting of some of the adult roles was less straightforward, and touched on a perennial problem for theatres in the National's bracket. By the spring, Michael Bryant and John Normington — two seasoned and valued members of the National company — had been pencilled in to play the Cardinal Inquisitor and the Pope respectively. These were small parts — each speaking in only a couple of scenes — but they needed to be played with great authority if Galileo's opposition was to be credible rather than caricatured. The same applied to other, even smaller roles — as Howard Brenton graphically put it, 'anyone in this play with ermine on his clothes is a killer.' Characters like the Pope, though, are difficult to cast. Actors from outside are unlikely to join to play one such role, and actors from within the company will only agree if the role is part of a satisfying programme of work. At the last minute, Bryant and Normington became unavailable. Bryant was required to film the National's production of *The Double Dealer* for Granada Television and Normington had long been promised leave of absence to direct a play at the Edinburgh Festival. Their schedules, it was discovered, clashed with rehearsals for *Galileo*. After some horse-trading — with actors being appointed to Cardinalships in a fashion that might have been recognisable behind the scenes at the Vatican itself — Basil Henson was cast as the Pope. The Cardinal Inquisitor proved a tougher nut to crack.

By this time, Dexter had sorted out most of the very smallest parts. It was not simply a matter of deciding which two or three roles would best suit which artiste. Logistical trickery was required to minimise audience recognition of the fact that the same actor was appearing more than once. Dexter explained, as

Marc Brenner at an early rehearsal for *Galileo*

an example, that the actor playing the Thin Monk – who denounces Galileo as a heretic in a couple of brief but powerful speeches – would make such an impact that he would have to be masked in the carnival and disguised in some other way if he were to be used elsewhere. The smallest roles had to be got absolutely right – Dexter called it the 'Button Moulder' syndrome. Some might think an outfit like the National was oversubscribed with personnel, but Dexter repeatedly complained that there was neither enough variety nor 'weight' among the 'lower orders'.

Dexter and casting director Gillian Diamond came closest to friction over the Cardinal Inquisitor. If ever a character needed 'weight', it was this ecclesiastical equivalent of the head of BOSS. At one stage, Diamond compiled a list of about fifty actors who might be recruited from outside for the church dignitaries, but to no avail. Those Dexter liked were either unavailable or, as when Eric Porter was offered the Cardinal Inquisitor, said no. The name of Stephen Moore, who had the advantage of being a member of the company, kept cropping up but Dexter resisted. Moore was a lean, light actor who looked about ten years younger than he was and had enjoyed his biggest hit in Alan Ayckbourn's *Bedroom Farce*. Howard Brenton said: 'The Inquisitor has gone *through* things to get to that office. Stephen Moore is a nice young man.' But Moore had been pressing the National to give him other than what he himself termed 'Stephen Moore parts'.

With rehearsals only days away, Dexter was desperate. He had thought of asking Hall to 'lean on' Paul Scofield to play the part, but Hall wasn't around. Dexter woke up one morning at 5 o'clock with the idea that Lindsay Anderson should do it, and this prompted a stream of fantasies about theatre directors who would make good Cardinal Inquisitors. In time he agreed to discuss the role with Stephen Moore.

Describing this meeting, Moore said:

'At first I was affected by knowing that Michael Bryant was to have played it. I thought my doing it was a silly idea. I told John I thought it was a silly idea, and he said he was glad I'd said that because it meant we met on common ground.'

But when the actor read from the script, he and Dexter discerned an approach they thought might make the casting work. Moore was formally offered the part and accepted, after Dexter promised not to keep saying in rehearsals: 'Michael Bryant would have done it like this. . . .' Of Moore, Dexter later said to Howard Brenton: 'Perhaps there's iron underneath.'

Many other members of his profession might have thought Stephen Moore had everything going for him. Well established at the National, he was the first actor every casting director thought of for a particular species of role. But the artistes who came together in the cast of *Galileo* all had different pressures on them and different purposes they hoped their appearance in the show might serve. Moore was constantly asking himself whether or not to stay on at the South Bank, assessing the parts offered against the possibility of driving up a dead end. 'I'd like to really get away from Stephen Moore parts and just rely on what I've picked up to do something different. Doing the same thing over and over is how you become a star but it's unsatisfactory to me.'

Week 9, Thursday

Dexter was sitting in the Green Room bar at lunchtime discussing this book with me, when the most savage blow – and the ostensible cause of the rehearsal postponement – occurred. Gillian Diamond appeared, her large eyes wider than usual. She took Dexter into the corridor and delivered news that left him 'shattered'. With rehearsals due to start on Monday, Peter Firth had just asked to be released from the cast. The actor had said his wife would be having a baby near the time the show went on and he wanted to be with her. But as Diamond pointed out, he must have known about this when he was sent his contract in April. Although Firth had never signed up, Diamond had had his verbal agreement and saw his dropping out as a breach of theatre practice. Given his reputation Dexter's mood remained calm, and soon he resumed his conversation with me. Others at the National were more outspoken.

The director left the theatre early that afternoon to pull himself together. He was profoundly disappointed and felt he had failed to get the actor to take himself seriously. 'But,' he said later, 'I told myself "That's that – no one's indispensable".'

The task now was to replace Firth – to find a first-rate actor at exceedingly short notice. Dexter said he would normally have spent two months recruiting his Andrea, but confessed that the practical problem was as nothing compared with the shock he had suffered.

Firth's agent later said that domestic pressures in addition to his wife's pregnancy had beset the actor at the time of his withdrawal. Dexter and the National had 'over-reacted' in assuming (as they did) that the rest of Firth's scheduled work at the theatre was now cancelled. Peter Firth, stressed his agent, was as upset about what had happened as everybody else.

Among the young actors whom Diamond now lined up to meet Dexter was Cambridge-educated Michael Thomas – a small, fair man with classically English good looks. He had recently been gracing the nation's television screens in the *Mallens* saga, and had scored some success as Romeo with the Old Vic Company. He was, he admitted, one of those theatre folk who tended to 'knock' the National. There was an additional complication, which caused Diamond to hope Dexter would reject him: Thomas was already committed to a television role, for which filming was about to start. But Dexter liked the actor and Diamond was landed with extricating him from the TV job. Having been let down by Firth, the National itself now prompted a tricky situation. In the event, the TV director told Diamond that if Thomas wanted to go to the National then he no longer wanted him for the TV role. A big scene had been averted, but everyone knew that – in terms of professional ethics – they had sailed close to the wind.

Thomas was philosophical about being Dexter's second choice. 'Laurence Olivier's the first choice for any part,' he said. And after the public previews of *Galileo* had begun, Dexter added this postscript: 'Michael Thomas is going to be extraordinary. And he's been less hard work than Peter would have been.'

Week 8, Wednesday

In the evening, Dexter and friends gathered at Jocelyn Herbert's small town house seeing themselves very much as a beleaguered

Michael Thomas
in rehearsal

group. The National in general and Hall in particular were the objects of a kind of despairing resentment. Peter Hartwell remarked that he did not know how Dexter had stuck at it. The play would take over in time, said the director philosophically. Howard Brenton arrived. The dramatist was a little *distrait* following a day at rehearsals for his anti-Tory satire *A Short Sharp Shock*, although the controversy that was to envelop this revue had not yet blown up. There was some honest-to-goodness gossip – about how Dexter had turned down *Evita*, for example – and a round of curses over the casting situation. Then helpings of 'Jocelyn's special' stew were consumed with several bottles of wine, and Dexter addressed everyone's attention to the thorny question they had come to discuss.

Brecht constantly reworked the final scene of *Galileo*, which was cut from the Berliner Ensemble's and many subsequent productions. The sequence revolves around Andrea. In the immediately preceding episode he has visited his disgraced former teacher and heard him lengthily condemn himself. Galileo also announces that he has finished his masterwork, the *Discorsi*, in secret. This causes Andrea to revise his opinion of Galileo and praise him for courageous pragmatism. But the physicist remains convinced that he should never have recanted and that if he had not, he would still have been able to complete his researches. In the contentious closing scene, Andrea is seen smuggling the *Discorsi* across the border for publication. Some children are denouncing a local old woman as a witch, and Andrea attempts to dislodge their superstitions. A slightly symbolic note is struck as, in the last lines of the play, Andrea portends the 'new age' and tells one of the boys: 'We don't know nearly enough. . . . We're really only at the beginning.' During their country sojourn, Dexter and Herbert had quarrelled over whether this scene should be included in their production. Herbert hated it, Dexter wasn't sure. But Howard Brenton had always been strongly in favour.

Now Dexter declared that his inclination was against. The sequence was badly written – Andrea's closing speech was 'Disney and sentimental' – and Brecht had never finally solved the scene's problems. Dexter wanted to take the visual image of the *Discorsi* crossing the border – which could look marvellous on the deep Olivier stage – and attach it to the end of the previous scene, where the ancient Galileo is left gobbling his food. The picture of the fallible human indulging his appetite appealed to Dexter because of its autobiographical resonance. He saw the play as a kind of unconscious autobiography, echoing compromises Brecht himself had made, for example, in order to thrive in post-war East Germany.

It was precisely in order to 'wipe out' this last image of Galileo that Brenton wanted to retain the fifteenth scene. 'The play should be about what Galileo *did*,' he stressed, 'not a personal tragedy.' Herbert interposed: 'It's about a man – a man's tragedy. Galileo was right to condemn himself.' Brenton argued that he was wrong to condemn himself. 'He gave us the modern world, but he also gave us the problems of the modern world.' Brenton and Herbert agreed on this, but it emerged as the evening wore on that they differed as to how they saw the modern world.

Their efforts must, said Andy Phillips, get Brecht a good press. Brecht himself would have been concerned that, apart from *The Caucasian Chalk Circle*, he had never been well received in England. 'That's corrupt,' cried Brenton. 'Brecht would have said "How can I play that scene *and* get a good press?"' Brenton was similarly forthright throughout the debate. When someone drew analogies with *Moses and Aaron* and *Turandot* he snorted, 'This is rhetoric.' And when Phillips said that no actors would want to follow Gambon's long speech at the end of the penultimate scene, Brenton railed at 'the *mores* of our theatre'. They had a duty to make the scene work, he insisted.

Phillips countered that the play was 'pragmatic' all the way through, but that the scene in question was suddenly dogmatic and represented 'a minor anecdote'. He suggested Brenton write a whole new scene, but Brenton and Dexter pointed out that the Brecht estate would never wear that. 'The words aren't there,' said the director, 'and you can't invent them.' With a gleam in his eye, the young dramatist said: 'I could sort of translate them better.' With Phillips, Herbert disliked the pedagogical tone of the scene. 'It's a matter of taking the theatrical high away,' said Brenton. 'It means killing the climax,' mumbled Phillips, and Herbert – obviously unhappy – added: 'It's boring, it's documentary.'

But steadfastly and almost alone, Brenton backed the scene.

'How someone lies to the border police, it's very interesting. You have to see, to experience the book going over the border. Books going over borders are very contemporary. Without the scene, people will think of Galileo at the end, not of his science.'

The conversation had been friendly, if blunt, but at this point Dexter snapped: 'Well, if you're going to say that, dear, you might as well not do the play at all.'

In the end, Dexter said that he would rehearse the sequence and decide depending on how it came over in action. It was a measure of the professionalism and good faith that informed their deliberations that Dexter later tackled the scene with feverish application. That evening, as Brenton and Phillips slipped away, Dexter and the others were left studying pictures of the galaxies for use in the slides. It was well past 11 o'clock.

Antagonism continued to surround the production. Dexter learned that little more than thirty performances were scheduled up to the projected end of the play's run in February. This squared with the National's estimate that they had a reliable audience of twenty to thirty thousand for something like *Galileo*, but it hardly appeared just reward for the monumental effort the show had already cost. Another blow was the discovery that Michael Gambon was committed to matinée performances on nearly half the Wednesdays and Saturdays of the rehearsal period. Although union regulations would allow Dexter a couple of hours with the actor in the morning, he would be reluctant to use them and would thus lose his leading man for the whole of each of these days. What was more, Gambon was in thirteen of the play's fifteen scenes! Dexter protested to Michael Elliott about the timetable, but it was by then too late to change it.

More strife arose over the number of rehearsals on stage Dexter was being offered. 'Let's use them all,' he had told his staff director, Kenneth Mackintosh, 'and see if we can get more.' Of the plays then in the repertoire, only *Othello* offered an acting area resembling that for *Galileo*: it would be impossible to rehearse when the set was up for other shows, and he could only rehearse on *Othello* days if no change-over was in progress. Another confrontation with Bill Bundy had failed to resolve the projection problem. But Herbert and Dexter had contributed to the economy drive by digging out six costumes, left over from *Volpone*, which they were prepared to use for the Venetian senate. Herbert didn't like the fur on the collars, but Dexter commented drily: 'Our colour scheme still has an organisation, even if it's not actually a colour scheme.'

During the weekend before rehearsals started, Dexter mapped out detailed movements for each scene – the 'blocking', or 'plumbing' as he called it, that would tell the story of the play. Nowadays, many see such advance planning by the director as an imposition. But Dexter believed – and a lot of the cast later concurred – that it would provide a basis of confidence for actors to develop their performances the more freely. Besides, the blocking could change as rehearsals progressed. Dexter habitually revised some before it reached the rehearsal floor, so as to eliminate his own left-hand bias.

He adhered to his mistrust of the final scene, and to his idea of the play as partially about Brecht – not Brecht as a 'cop-out', but as a survivor.

The production Dexter contemplated was as important as any he had ever done. It was his first after a major illness and the inevitable self-assessment this had prompted. He still suffered every time he became excited, and he tended to become excited whenever he rehearsed. He had resolved to use pain as a warning sign of the need to calm down. Over and above this, there was the question of his professional future. He adored music, but directing opera was just not the same as directing theatre. He had been away from London for a long time: how many doors would remain open to him if *Galileo* were no more successful than *As You Like It*? He had recently let it be known through Herbert to some of her fellow members of the Royal Court board that he would be interested in returning there. A young director with a 'fringe' background, Max Stafford-Clark, was now running a chronically under-funded operation in Sloane Square, but his appointment was – formally, at any rate – only for a year. Dexter faced a drawback in that to many of the Court's present staff – indeed, to a few of its board – he was a name rather than a known quantity. As for the National – which he had once come so close to running – would his relationship with Hall, and his projected schedule of productions, survive the current tribulations?

If, as he had forecast, the play was going to take over, this would begin on Monday. Then the actors would get their hands on it at last. He would demand a 'hard, bright, fast' delivery. He would urge them to act 'honestly and without decoration'. The cast might not be as weighty as he would have liked, and the design depleted, but the master would be making no more compromises.

Chapter Six

First rehearsals

Week 7, Monday

Rehearsal Room 2 was gaunt and cavernous, like a television studio. On the floor, tape marked out the playing areas, and at one end steps led up to a wooden viewing platform. Dexter had originally asked for a temporary stage to be constructed as well, but this had been dropped in the economy measures at a saving of over £2,000. Along the walls hung floor-plans for each scene, and miscellaneous notices including an advertisement for 'flu vaccinations. By the door a telephone flashed a silent red light instead of ringing, and a microphone enabled the stage managers to page the building for missing personnel. High up on one of the black-painted walls someone had taped the word 'ASIDE'. It had been put up for an earlier show, and nobody knew what it meant, but it hovered enigmatically throughout the rehearsals for *Galileo*. The room was bleak and a little cold, and one would not have been surprised to see mist clinging to the ceiling.

Actors out of costume do not look like actors. Indeed, the sort of actors who get cast as senators, astronomers, monks and Lords Chamberlain tend, at rehearsals, to resemble estate agents and supermarket managers in their Saturday clothes. It was a rather motley, suburban crowd, then, whom Dexter surprised by announcing – promptly at 10.30 – that a 'warm-up' session was about to take place. 'You all know why Gordon's here,' he said of the compact figure at his side. That was plainly not the case, but the actors spread out willingly as the precisely-spoken voice coach eased them into some physical jerks.

As an actor, Gordon Gardner had played opposite such illustrious figures as Peter Finch and Vivien Leigh, but nowadays he spent more and more time teaching. The National's resident voice expert had died in 1978 and Gardner had been brought in on a freelance basis for *As You Like It*. Pre-occupied with audibility in the Olivier, Dexter had asked for him again. Gardner saw his job, not as giving elocution lessons, but as 'tuning up the actors' instruments', and helping them release their vocal energy efficiently under the stress of performance. He sat in on nearly every rehearsal, taking actors to one side on occasion and offering some of them individual sessions. On this first morning, he soon had the assembled actors raising and lowering their arms like marionettes, breathing in and out while counting, repeating 'wee, why, woe' louder and softer and louder again, jumping up and down, loosening their shoulders, and exclaiming 'Bash!'

Even if they still looked nonplussed, at least they were beginning to sound like actors, with Gambon's voice booming prominently. The star-to-be was lost in the middle of the crowd, Stephen Moore lurked near the back, while Marc Brenner and veteran actor Andrew Cruickshank were close together at the front. Gardner urged them to repeat 'Bash!', punching the air, then to stretch and make shrinking movements. Asking them to lie down, he said gently: 'Sorry if you're wearing your pretty clothes, but you deserve a rest.' Dexter chimed in 'Wrong!' and began to patrol the prostrate bodies.

'This is where I like you,' said the director, 'at my feet!' Cruickshank and Harry Lomax – the National's longest-serving artiste – had fallen into chairs rather than on to the floor. Dexter approached Cruickshank, not to tick him off but to massage his back. The actor chuckled benignly. The atmosphere was pregnant – something about Dexter always suggested a brewing storm – but the laughter was frequent and more than simply nervous.

Gathering them round the model of the set, Dexter explained that there would be voluntary voice classes for the first half-hour of every morning. He wanted 'all the vocal precision, intensity and excitement of a Shakespearean production'. Gluttony was an important theme in the play and this needed to be matched by 'a positively Shakespearean relish of the text'. In a brisk talk, he touched but did not dwell on his preferred notion of the play. 'My approach might be heretical, but if it's

Gordon Gardner (arm outstretched) leads the 'warm-up' at the first rehearsal

'This is where I like you,' said the director, 'at my feet!'

heretical like Tyrone Guthrie's *Henry VIII* I won't mind and neither will the Brecht estate.'

The play presented, he said, a life of Galileo that made a point about responsibility. It also contained, 'a little unbeknownst to Brecht', a point about survival. Read one of the biographies, suggested Dexter, to find out about Brecht's struggles to keep his theatres open. And now they must get on. Before tea he had to get through the first four scenes – over an hour of playing time – as the boy actors involved would be off taking exams next day. Indicating the set he said: 'If you don't know why we've got a square on a circle, go back to elementary physics – that's not my job,' and then announced a fifteen-minute coffee break.

Piled high in the corners of the room were furniture and 'props' that looked finished but were in fact only for rehearsals. Tables, chairs, rostra, and telescopes were swiftly moved into place by the stage managers when required. At one point, a switch was thrown and a large section of one wall slid sideways. This revealed a long, bright corridor where the actors seldom went – it led to the workshops – and yet more well-worn, apparently authentic seventeenth-century furniture was carried in.

Dexter easily got through the first four scenes. With an hour off for lunch, rehearsals were over by 4.27. He knew what he wanted in each passage, but was also quick to change what he was asking for. Not having walls with doors in the set, he was particularly busy determining where exits would be and where they would lead. Herbert was on hand, and he would sometimes defer to her advice on the stage picture. He showered the actors with large moves and suggestions for the tiniest pieces of 'business'. These they devoured like hungry children, scribbling them into their large red-bound scripts. Gambon alternated between a rapid, deadpan reading – his head down, his movements slightly restless – and occasional stabs at full-blown performance. From the start, Andrew Cruickshank, as the university bursar whom Galileo tricks by pretending he has invented the telescope, gave a much fuller essay than most of the others. His ringing Highland tones inevitably reminded one of his appearances in *Dr Finlay's Casebook*, and he had a unique method of babbling miscellaneously but convincingly while waiting for a prompt. Marc Brenner, loyally sporting a National Theatre

Above Dexter's first
day address to the cast.
On his left is the model
of the set

Left Tiny replicas
of furniture and
characters that
accompanied the set
model

sweater, conducted himself with discreet efficiency, as if he had spent his life in rehearsal rooms.

At lunchtime, the artistes teemed into the staff canteen. Here the fare was basic and cheap, but a rich view was available of St Paul's, the towers of the City of London, and busy building sites along the banks of the river. Actors great and humble joined the queue at the self-service counter, sometimes in costume, sometimes in plain clothes. Along with dinner-jacketed waiters off duty from the front-of-house restaurant, ushers wearing natty brown smocks and National Theatre neck-scarves, and kitchen staff in their bright orange outfits, they brought welcome relief to the anonymity of the canteen décor. (All this costume made life difficult for the theatre chaplain, who could never persuade people his own uniform was *bona fide*.)

The mood of the cast was optimistic. Gambon talked briefly with Alan Ayres from the press office. The actor enjoyed being rude, but his ingenuous manner – matched by a pasty face and slightly dishevelled appearance – was such that he never gave offence. 'Are you doing the publicity on this show?' he asked. When Ayres said he was, Gambon muttered: 'That means there won't *be* any publicity then.' The remark was to have an ironic reverberation eight weeks later.

Gambon shunned personal publicity. He felt he was bad at talking about himself, and had seen other actors make fools of themselves in print when they should have kept quiet. People's ideas about an actor, gleaned from the press, could get between them and a performance. 'In that sense,' said Gambon, 'an actor should be mysterious.' He was once telephoned by a reporter while rehearsing 'one of those terrible television comedies I do'. The journalist said: 'I'm from the *Sun*. Is that Michael Gambon?' The actor replied 'No, I'm the assistant floor manager,' and put the phone down.

He had enjoyed the first day's work. Dexter's blocking was 'wonderful'. He did not have a lot of profound thoughts about the part. He seemed concerned about people's dislike for Brecht, and he was not the first to commend the 'playability' of Brenton's translation. The play ought to be funny, thought Gambon, 'a laugh a line'. Far from losing any sleep, he had nearly been late for rehearsals that morning.

Gambon added, perhaps unsurprisingly, that he was approaching Galileo as 'just another part'. By contrast, Elliott Cooper was thinking about his performance very much in terms of career. Soon after drama school, he had landed a sizeable part in the film *Aces High* but this had been followed by seven months out of work. He had then been in panto at Sidmouth, and played a servant in a dreadful tour of *Romeo and Juliet* during which he discovered to his consternation that he was expected to help shift scenery as well. He ended up as stage assistant to the puppet Basil Brush. After two years at the National, he had made little headway. In fact, he had given notice and was being phased out of the repertoire when Dexter offered him Lodovico. Cooper decided to stay, but planned to invite plenty of producers and casting directors to see his performance. This was not out of disloyalty to the National: he had, he said, no way of knowing whether other directors in the building were saying 'Who's this no-talent John's given a part to?' or 'This looks interesting, let's see how Elliott gets on.' Performances are tender, he explained, with which actors hope to purchase work in the future.

An older member of the cast was thinking less strategically. Gordon Whiting had been in the profession longer than Cooper's twenty-eight-year life, but apart from understudying Iago his roles at the National had also been small. As an adversary of Galileo's at the Florentine court, he was being urged by Dexter not to 'comment' on his character nor play him from Galileo's point of view. Whiting had had larger roles in London: a year in the lead in *The Mousetrap* was followed by six-and-a-half years in *No Sex Please We're British*. But the National was attractive because the plays were interesting. He had, he said, looked back on whole decades of his career and decided he had not been in a single play worth doing. But he was no more thin-skinned than Cooper. He characterised himself as one of a group in the cast of *Galileo* whom he called 'older boys'. Whiting expounded philosophically:

'We've played leads in rep, maybe even juvenile leads, and the fact that we're here now playing small parts means we've not made the grade as we'd like to have done. If you've not played big parts with good people, you lose confidence. Confidence makes you a better actor. Perhaps when I was thirty, I was a better actor than I am now.'

Dexter ploughed tirelessly through the play during this first week. Gardner drilled the company with increasing vigour and distributed sheets of exercises to be tried out at home. Movements were made with appropriate sounds – 'bend', 'crush', 'smash' – and emotions were expressed – 'surprise', 'horror', 'joy' – first thing every morning. During work on a scene outside the Collegium Romanum, where Galileo and assorted opponents await the Papal Astronomer's verdict on the new discoveries, Dexter pounced quickly on individuals. Artro Morris, playing a Fat Monk who denounces Galileo's ideas with aggressive horseplay, was told not to 'act fat'; and young Adam Norton, as the more grimly fanatical Thin Monk, was urged not to shout – so confident should his character be in his century-old beliefs that he 'must have no voice at all'. Basil Henson knew most of his lines at the first rehearsal, and offered quite a rounded performance as the Cardinal who becomes Pope. Stephen Moore, on the other hand, was playing in a very low key, and Gambon experimented almost surreptitiously. Attention to detail was already the order of the day. Herbert was brought in to discuss the kind of chair on which Galileo might lift the boy Andrea as he demonstrates the earth's movement round the sun, and a number were tried. And during a formal ball sequence, a protracted discussion developed about exactly how Lodovico would hold out his hand toward his fiancée.

Week 7, Friday

By the end of the week, astonishingly, they were ready to 'run through' most of the play. Dexter told the cast at the outset that nobody would be watching the acting but they should 'try to get the moves right and be clear.' The object was for him and Herbert to see if the plumbing was basically right, and for Gambon 'to get some sense of the journey and how long it is.' The red-headed figure of Kevin Leeman from the music department perched at the piano, and everyone was taken aback by the length of Hans Eisler's musical introductions to each scene.

The rehearsal occasionally soared, and was almost always confident: only the precise location of exits and entrances caused confusion. Gambon was relaxed and giggly at times. He

Rehearsal Room 2 (right) seen from the workshops corridor

An early rehearsal of the scene in which Galileo hears that a
mathematician is to become Pope and resumes his forbidden
researches. *Left to right:* Michael Gambon (Galileo), John Dexter,
Simon Callow (the Little Monk), Michael Thomas (seated, Andrea
as a man) and James Hayes (Federzoni, another of Galileo's disciples).

seemed determined not to give a performance and lost his way in an early speech proclaiming the 'new age'. The university bursar's name – Priuli – was given a remarkable variety of pronunciations. Dexter prowled the narrow viewing gallery, animatedly discussing the lay-out of scenes with Herbert, gesticulating at the stage managers if ever a piece of furniture was in the wrong place. After the lunch break, James Hayes, whom Dexter had asked to be brought into the company especially to play Galileo's disciple Federzoni, was absent when everyone else was ready for the next scene. He was 'tannoyed' three times. Tension appeared for the first time that week as Dexter became increasingly agitated. The actor arrived a couple of minutes late and Dexter said quietly: 'Come on Jimmy, we're all waiting for you and have been for five minutes.' As Hayes took his place, Dexter suddenly spotted that publicist Alan Ayres had slipped in to talk to one of the cast not involved with the scene in hand. 'Clear the room please,' he cried out. 'Excuse me, you're not required.' Ayres left hurriedly. As the scene got under way, Michael Thomas knocked over a blackboard and Dexter snapped at stage manager John Rothenberg: 'I want that making secure.' But this glimpse of the Dexter of repute did not last long, his temper soothed no doubt by the impressiveness of the later scenes. In one ceremonial sequence, the Pope is dressed while arguing over Galileo's fate with the Cardinal Inquisitor. The team of attendants were so tightly choreographed they might have been rehearsing nothing else all week. At the end, Dexter said thoughtfully: 'Thank you. Very well done. It'll never be as bad as that again, and some of it will never be as good, unfortunately.'

Far from congratulating himself, Dexter bubbled with ideas for improvements and changes after the run. He would drop the plague sequence as it was 'interrupting the flow of the narrative'. This brought their version of the play down to fourteen scenes. The interval would be placed earlier to help separate the more discursive scenes. Dexter intended to clarify the plumbing even more, especially the doors in Galileo's house, differentiating between upstairs and down, outdoors and in. 'They're beginning to get the point that it's witty,' he said, 'I'll be developing that.' But he had not liked the laughs early in the Collegium Romanum scene. The writing, he felt, was naïve.

The 'Pope dressing' ritual rehearsed: Basil Henson (as the Pope) is the only one sitting down!

Yvonne Bryceland (script in hand) rehearses with Selina Cadell

There was a danger the audience would view as merely silly the priests and astronomers who decry Galileo. More grained performances from Artro Morris, Adam Norton *et al.* might have made him feel differently, but he had decided to cut the first page and start the scene on a more earnest note.

Earlier in the week he had discouraged Yvonne Bryceland, as Galileo's long-suffering housekeeper, from giving an 'off' (or exaggerated-working class) characterisation: now he needed to rebuild the performance with a series of pointed questions about the character's life. As Virginia, Selina Cadell had to travel from an optimistic teenagehood to disappointed middle age; about her work, Dexter said: 'Selina's terrified of the plunge into the ageing process. She's got to see there's nothing wrong with making a bold dash early. This play is like revue, there's no time to sense your way through a part.'

Gambon had found the run useful, despite feeling 'awful – like a wooden dummy saying lines.' He tended to approach performances, like Olivier, by way of externals and he was already preoccupied with how old and/or fat Galileo should appear at different points in the play. He was glad to discover he had a spell off-stage – while Galileo is a guest of the Inquisition – which he had earmarked for the final phase of 'ageing'.

Moving off for the weekend, Dexter was restless and concentrated at the same time. He carried a clutch of sketches, made during the run in place of the usual written notes, which he would be scrutinising before Monday. He must start work now, he said, having got it 'fifty per cent right'. Underneath it all, he seemed rather happy.

Chapter Seven

Work in progress

It was not until Week 7 that answers were found to the outstanding design questions. Before the production meeting, Bill
Bundy's team had thought that the back projector would be
located in the rear stage beyond the metal shutters. Dexter's
demand for a 'surround' across the back of the stage put paid to
that, since the surround would come between the projector and
screen. The solution arrived at was to build a special platform
for the projector, suspended high up immediately in front of
the central metal shutter. From here, an image could be thrown
at an angle over the top of the surround and down on to the
screen. In order to give a symmetrical image, the slides would
need to be printed with a distortion, and Mark Taylor set about
calculating this exactly. It was then realised that the platform
idea obviated the need for the expensive surround altogether. A
big argument for masking the shutters with a surround was that
the central shutter would need to be raised to allow for the
projecting, so, without masking, the audience would be able to
see into the rear stage. With the projector in front, the shutter
could remain lowered during the show. In fact, it would be
lowered all but the last few feet, where the false, soundless
shutter would operate to allow the truck to come through. Some
thought Dexter's surround idea had been a ploy to get his way
over the shutters. If so, the ploy had worked.

Bill Bundy managed to arrange the loan of two back projectors from the Royal Opera House, where he had worked for
many years. It turned out that to buy each would have cost
nearer £7,000 than the £5,000 estimated at the production meeting. But this did not solve all the projection problems. For the
very end of the play, Dexter had asked for a panorama of stars to
appear across the back of the stage. As Andrea departs, the

director wanted one of the boys he has been addressing to watch this galaxy, symbolising all the as yet uncharted areas of knowledge to which Andrea has referred. To produce a strong image on the shutters – given that some, at least, of Andy Phillips's bright white lighting would be in use – proved no easy matter. A scheme was adopted involving three more huge projectors, but it was not worked out until after rehearsals had started, and was the cause of more strife between Dexter and Bundy.

As Jocelyn Herbert's plans became more difficult to effect, so the picture they were to offer became simpler. At the very back would be seen the metal shutters. Nearer the audience, the skeletal aluminium framework would hold the screen, which could be raised and lowered. Immediately in front of this, the raised disc provided the principal playing area and was effectively the centrepiece of the design. The disc could be reached from the wings and rear stage by ramps, and from the stalls by steps in the centre aisle and the 'vomitories' at either side. The musicians and a choir would sit in a box at one side of the auditorium; opposite would perch the prompter and a character called The Speaker, who would introduce each scene to the audience. For the 'interior' scenes, the truck would travel from the rear stage beneath the aluminium framework and on to the disc. Very little conventional décor was to be used. To identify the Collegium Romanum a huge portal would be positioned before the framework. In front of this, the Thin Monk and others would berate Galileo, and it provided the Papal Astronomer with a magnificent entrance at the climax of the scene when he arrives to announce that Galileo's findings are valid. For the following scene, in which cardinals fête the scientist but warn him off his more controversial researches, a balustrade would appear just behind the framework. Most of the remaining scenic effects were to be achieved by the judicious use of furniture. As Jocelyn Herbert remarked, the overall impression would be markedly spare considering the effort expended.

Responsible for making a smoothly functioning reality of all this were the backstage staff. At the National, they were divided into two groups. The 'stage' departments – including stage management, scene shifters, sound and lighting experts – worked on shows at the time of performance. The 'workshop' departments, housed across the way from Rehearsal Room 2, constructed sets, props and so on in advance of performance. At least, they were supposed to be made in advance. Bits of scenery had been hammered into place minutes before the official first nights of quite recent productions – this, of course, was the kind of thing the 22-week cycle had been brought in to combat.

Co-ordinating backstage work is customarily the task of a theatre's production manager. The National employed a production manager, with assistants, for each of its auditoria. Working from an office on the fourth floor of the building, these people were Bill Bundy's immediate deputies, and their jobs combined donkey work with administration. The Olivier's production manager would normally have been one of Jocelyn Herbert's chief contacts at the National. Not long before *Galileo* went into production, however, the man concerned gave notice. Finding a replacement proved very difficult. Bill Bundy's confidence in the assistant production manager, twenty-five-year-old Mark Taylor, was not exactly boundless. Instead of promoting Taylor, Bundy caused some upset by moving Rodger Hulley over to act as Olivier production manager while maintaining the same position in the Lyttelton. As it happened, Mark Taylor and Rodger Hulley got on well together. But their evident youth – barely disguised by fashionable moustaches – did not always help them deal with others when matters were at their most weighty. Another innovation of Bundy's had perturbed them both. In March 1980, a workshops manager had been appointed. He was placed in charge of all the workshop departments, which thereby lost some autonomy, and he took over some of the co-ordinating functions that had previously been performed by the production managers.

The tensions that were bound to be stirred by this move were exacerbated by the chemistry of personalities. The new appointee was John Malone, a chubby Northerner with an exceptionally dry sense of humour. Before coming to the National, he had been in charge of a commercial scenery construction business with a staff of fifty, owned by Trident Television. Having earlier worked in theatre, he came close to satisfying the National's near-impossible job specification. As Bill Bundy put it, their workshops operated on the scale of a factory, and this necessitated a manager with broader experience than that of most theatre people.

Paradoxically, one of the complaints of workshop heads – such as Yves Rassou, the softly spoken Mauritian in charge of the paint frame – was that Malone ran things too much like a factory. Rassou and most of his seven-strong staff had trained as visual artists; as such, he explained, they would often work past 1 o'clock in the afternoon if something dissatisfied them, and would consequently return from lunch later than 2 o'clock. Rassou would then find himself quizzed as to whether his people had been stringing out their breaks. Malone's television background did not endear him to others. Carpenters Doug and Alan Sutton, for example, found most TV scenery so imperfect as to make viewing painful. In the face of such mistrust, Malone was determined to improve communication between work-shops, break down suspicion of cost accounting, and to save – as he reckoned he could in a year – a six-figure sum.

One of his earliest clashes with Taylor on *Galileo* concerned the substructure that would hold up the 'floating disc'. Tra-ditionally, this would comprise wooden rostra, but Malone decreed that steel supports should be constructed under Eric Dunn's supervision in the National's metal works. To Dunn's chagrin, the more challenging truck was being made by Kemp's, but he acknowledged that his shop was under-equipped for that job at the time.

The flooring for the disc and its attendant ramps took a fort-night to build in the carpentry shop, where John Phillips over-saw a staff of nineteen. Then scaffolding boards had to be readied to cover the truck. Jocelyn Herbert had asked specifically for scaffolding boards, which are usually rough sawn, but when these were being painted she noticed a slightly dark pattern caused by saw marks. She asked for the board to be fine planed to eliminate the marks, and they then had to be repainted and later waxed. John Phillips said: 'The boy I got to do the planing took a week over it. He failed to understand why it needed doing, since he couldn't see the marks from ten feet away. I had to explain the particular quality Jocelyn was looking for.'

Meanwhile, Doug and Alan Sutton were building the portal for the Collegium Romanum, little realising how troublesome a piece of scenery this would prove to be.

Assistant production
manager Mark Taylor
with one of the
projectors borrowed
from the Royal Opera
House

John Malone (left, the
new workshops
manager) with John
Phillips (in charge of
the carpentry
workshop)

Carpentry is carried out in pairs – two people to a bench – and is very much a family trade. But the Suttons were unusual in being a father-and-son team. They could easily match Jocelyn Herbert for perfectionism. They preferred theatre to the building trade, said Alan Sutton, because they avoided 'brickies and plumbers who rip up your work'. They eschewed short cuts, such as rubber moulding which might have cut down the week they spent on the portal. Each job was unique. The same item of scenery would be made differently for different theatres under the National roof depending on fireproofing regulations, which scene shifters would be handling it, and a host of other factors. The portal – which for some reason became known as the 'Rome door' – was a solid, three-dimensional piece of carpentry representing a stone arch and wooden doorway. The painted canvas 'flats' of convention were only one of many scenic media in the National's repertoire.

The carpenters' shop and paint frame were easily the largest rooms in the building, apart from the auditoria. The 'Rome door' was in time moved through their connecting metal partition into Rassou's domain. Here a variety of techniques were exercised to achieve the surface and texture – not merely the colour – demanded by the designer. Some workshop staff criticised Herbert for the time she took over decisions, but Rassou's team – fellow artists of hers – appreciated the initiative bestowed on them whenever she said, 'You know what I mean . . .'

Rassou's colleague Hazel Gash spent two-and-a-half days on the 'Rome door'. She covered it with a sawdust and glue mixture first, then Toupret (a substance not unlike Polyfilla but creamier), followed by two coats of paint. Similarly, the plywood sheets provided by the carpenters for the disc floor were given a basic texture with plaster and sawdust, a thin layer of latex for sound-proofing, a coat of paint and lastly a glaze. The grooves between them were then roughened and broken to give a final effect remarkably like weather-beaten paving stones. It had taken a week of experiments to come up with a specimen surface that Herbert approved, and the painters were perfectly prepared for her to demand more changes when she saw the finished article under Andy Phillips's lights.

Clinging like ears to either side of the carpenters' shop and paint frame were the smaller workshops which made up the rest

Doug Sutton with the portal or 'Rome door'

of John Malone's empire: the armoury, metal works, and props department.

Barry Saltman's three-strong corps of armourers – he described them sardonically as 'the equivalent of one-and-a-half men' – were responsible for decorative metalwork and pyrotechnics such as guns and shells, as well as the armour, swords and pikes of which they had an awesome collection. Sharing quarters with Eric Dunn's team, they inhabited the least 'theatrical' pocket of the National. Dunn was a gnomic Liverpudlian who learnt his trade during seven years in the army. A photo of himself with the National Theatre football team, various rosettes, a battered first-aid cupboard, *Machinery's Handbook* and *Who's Who In Shakespeare* crammed the dusty shelves round his office desk. Here his 'metal beauticians' would take their tea breaks – three fully qualified welders, and one apprentice. Eighteen-year-old Stephen Burrows from Sydenham was, they believed, the only welder in the country serving his apprenticeship at a theatre. There had been forty-two applicants for his position, and Dunn was delighted with him. His comrades included Lee Stalker-Clarke, a mechanical engineer who had only seen one live show before joining the National, and Sylvia Starshine. Starshine was one of the USA's first peacetime female welders and had come to Britain to work on the reconstruction of an iron age farm at Petersfield. Needing to subsidise herself, she applied for the job with Dunn. She also took to science fiction illustrating, and adopted her exotic name to help her get on in that over-subscribed field. This group's responsibility was for structural – rather than ornamental – metalwork. Dunn pointed out that they offered the National more than their official qualifications: he had acted on occasion as an informal military advisor, and Starshine, who was a medievalist, once taught an actress how to spin. They gave a sense of cheer in the face of adversities, such as the 'rapidly breeding' substructure, and drawings which – had they not been quick to query them – would have led to some very odd-shaped steps leading up to the disc. 'Contrary to popular belief,' said Dunn unmaliciously, 'fitter welders can think.'

At the opposite end of the corridor worked the more 'aesthetic' members of the props department. Most of the dozen

In the paint frame, Hazel Gash (left) and Yves Rassou work on the flooring for the disc

people here had an art college background – some, indeed, had trained in theatre design. They were officially divided into 'makers' – the larger group – and 'buyers', but these distinctions were beginning to break down as individuals were encouraged to concentrate on whole shows. Most of the makers spent five or six weeks exclusively on *Galileo*; then, as other productions began to impinge at the end of June, three were left full-time, two part-time.

Demarcation over props was something of an enigma. The props team were responsible for items like cigarettes and matches that might elsewhere be obtained by stage management; but upstairs in the wardrobe a costume accessories department made things that might elsewhere be classified as props. Sometimes, who made what at the National would be decided by whichever department the designer in question had greater confidence in. For *Galileo*, masks to be worn by the dignitaries at the ball were made by costume accessories; masks and hobby horses used by the plebeians in the carnival were made by props. They had at first been given drawings for 7 masks, but Dexter – busily 'disguising' actors – asked for more, and they ended up putting together 4 hobby horses and about 20 masks. Each rough-looking mask took at least a day to make, then had to be 'fitted' to the actor concerned. The department was used to this sort of escalation in their work load, but would sometimes keep finished props away from rehearsals if they feared they would be asked to make unreasonable changes. Throughout the summer, props staff worked every weekend; in the last nine months of 1979, some of them had come in literally every day. One of the department heads commented: 'The only way you knew it was Sunday was that you got in quicker because there was less traffic about.' When they received timetables of 22-week cycles and such like, they just laughed; they were, they felt, very much 'the poor relations'.

But they welcomed the challenge of *Galileo* with its abundance of ancient scientific gear: three of them had spent several days researching at the Science Museum. And in common with Yves Rassou, they liked Jocelyn Herbert because of the room to manoeuvre she allowed them. The regard was reciprocated, but on one occasion Herbert concluded she had left too much room. David Allen was a newcomer to the team. Almost his first job

Chief of the 'metal beauticians', Eric Dunn. He is holding a model
of the 'armillery sphere' which, suspended over the stage, was to
greet the audience on their arrival for *Galileo*

was to make the throne on which the Pope briefly perches during the ritual of his dressing. This project ended up dragging out over an agonising six weeks. The main difficulty was getting the throne the right colour. Allen first primed it with red oxide paint such as is used on cars; then coloured it with Dutch metal leaf (a microscopically thin foil used as an alternative to the more expensive gold leaf); covered it with French Enamel Varnish of varying shades, and sponged it over with meths. The result was a bright crimson finish that appalled Herbert when she saw it. Allen might have felt rueful about the initiative he had shown, but took the setback philosophically. He was obliged to take meths to the great chair again, apply Toupret to break up the pattern, and finally apply more metal leaf and French Enamel Varnish before the designer was satisfied. Then the cushion was covered with bedspread material bought cheap from a shop behind Liverpool Street Station. It had begun life as an orangey-brown, been dyed for use in another production, had then been bleached, re-dyed, and had French Enamel Varnish and other matter worked into it to create a texture of sufficient age and luxuriance for the papal posterior. Despite this elaborate trouble, material which looked the same when new would have cost a lot more.

The irony of Allen's finding himself in the dog house over *Galileo* was that he was a great Brecht fan, and had designed the show as a project during training at Wimbledon College. Not, he averred, that he would ever dream of offering suggestions to Herbert or any of the other designers.

Ever since the production meeting in Week 9, Herbert had been working full-time at the National. Far from her job finishing when the designs were settled on, she was engaged in a ceaseless round of consultations with workshop and costume department staff, and of attendance at rehearsals and costume fittings. Even so, many backstage personnel found her elusive. The fact that drawings had been delayed and that the theatre had not yet fully evolved its production system under John Malone made for a series of muddles, especially in the armoury, whose chief, Barry Saltman, was also coping with domestic difficulties.

First, Saltman bought brass and made stands for a canopy that would shelter the Venetian senate; he was told these were too heavy and could not be used. Then a brass telescope was

Lee Stalker-Clarke (left) and colleague in the metal workshop

Sylvia Starshine

made within two days of his receiving a drawing; this time, he was informed that wooden or even cardboard telescopes were to be made by the props team and covered with leather. Saltman agreed this was a better idea, but claimed that the job specification had been for brass.

Next his crew were asked to make a sundial, on the basis of a drawing which Herbert thought was sufficient but which Saltman found inadequate. When Galileo is with the Inquisition, his disciples are told that a bell will ring at five o'clock to signal his recantation. Poring over the sundial, they watch the time pass five and assume that he has not recanted. They begin to celebrate, then the bell – a little late – chimes. The sundial's appearance is brief, then, but important. Having made it, one of Saltman's staff spent three days intricately engraving its face. When Herbert eventually came to look at the sundial – 'three weeks later, after I'd been on and on at her for more details', according to Saltman – she was dissatisfied. It had been made to fit a flat plinth, but the plinth that had been constructed by another department was tilted; when the dial was positioned, it was double tilted and looked ridiculous. The designer also wanted it thicker, so the metal sheets were fixed to a timber disc and inevitably distorted. In the end, the job was re-commissioned outside and a new model went into the show on the last public preview. Herbert insisted that had she been asked more questions she would have responded, and supplied further drawings. But Saltman blamed the very 'freedom' that others appreciated. 'She is an artist and works better with artists than artisans.'

By contrast, Bill Bundy said that responsibility for the botchups over drawings lay not with Jocelyn Herbert but with the theatre and the growing pains of its new production methods.

The biggest bugbear of all for Saltman and his lieutenant, twenty-four-year-old Rob Barham, was the candelabra at the centre of Herbert's design for the ball sequence. There had been much discussion as to whether this should be genuine steel, in which case it would need to be made outside, or made of wood and painted. On the one hand, according to Herbert's philosophy, authenticity was important; on the other, the candelabra had to be easily lifted during scene-changes. Eventually work started on a model which, Barham estimated, would weigh up

Props workshop: Sue
Dunlop (right) works
on the head of a great
model of Galileo which
would appear at the
climax of the carnival
scene; to her left is
Richard Pocock

David Allen and the
controversial papal
throne

to 700lbs and cost over £1,000. He and others worked on this for a week, then Barham went on holiday. He returned to discover that it had been replaced by another, much lighter model. He and his colleagues worked on this for several more weeks, although they were not convinced it would ever arrive on stage. Leaf pressings had twice been applied and removed at Herbert's request. This left Barham – an undemonstrative and dedicated man, who had spent £4,500 of his own money building up a collection of over 500 tools – feeling that *Galileo* was 'a right crap show'. The armoury staff had not turned out work to be proud of, and they knew it.

Meanwhile, Eric Dunn was grappling with another set-piece. This was a huge armillery sphere to greet the audience on their arrival in the auditorium. Metal circles were to be brought from outside, but welded together in Dunn's shop. These hoops had been promised for 30 June, and the finished article was scheduled to be positioned above the stage a month later. By 2 July, no delivery had been made and Dunn had a nasty suspicion that the suppliers might be expecting him to collect. He telephoned them that afternoon.

As John Malone continued to process *Galileo* through his workshops, Rodger Hulley and Mark Taylor looked on with scepticism. Indeed, they were pretty sceptical a lot of the time. But it would be wrong to see them as maintaining a tradition of backstage recalcitrance. They had reasonable grievances. Directors of theatres are usually directors of plays. Efficient systems set in motion by directors in their executive capacity could be overridden by the same directors on artistic grounds. Hulley and Taylor held to the unromantic belief that shows that kept on schedule were in the end better shows. Most people said it had been worse in the past, but the workshops were again experiencing their annual summer pile-up. (Doug Sutton had joined the National carpenters' shop in the expectation of not working overtime; in five years, he had only worked the standard forty hours for six or seven weeks.)

The Olivier created unusual problems. Without the framework of the proscenium, directors and designers found it harder to make up their minds. They also tended to change their minds more often. This was because the National, unlike smaller outfits, tried to get scenery and props in front of them before it

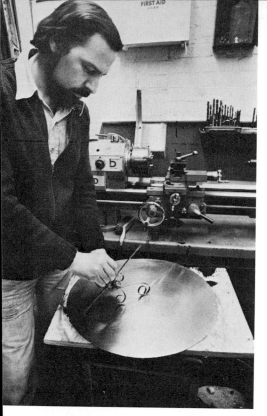

Armourer Barry
Saltman with a
prototype of the
sundial

Rob Barham
surrounded by his
collection of tools

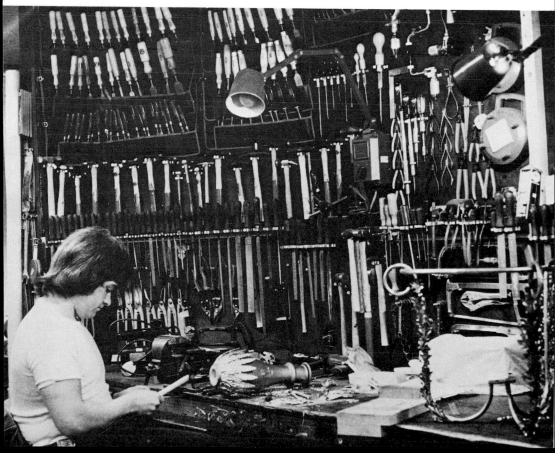

was too late to make changes. And whatever they wanted to do had to be negotiated with the fire brigade, the electrical and architectural departments of the Greater London Council, and even – because of the projection platform built specially for *Galileo* – with the district surveyor for the London Borough of Lambeth. During the production week of *Undiscovered Country* in the Olivier, Mark Taylor had worked 102 hours. He hoped – but faintly – that *Galileo* would be different. And Dexter was back. Things were moving, but he predicted a storm would break soon.

While *Galileo* preoccupied the 'workshop' departments, most of the 'stage' departments were busy with other productions. The exception to the rule that 'stage' departments were not active on a show until Week 0 was the stage management team. Its boss, John Rothenberg, was a dapper, neatly bearded Australian, and another old chum of Dexter's, having worked with him at the Vic. At the ideal performance, said Rothenberg, the audience would be unaware of his staff's contribution. They ran rehearsals with a similar seamlessness, in the face of mountainous logistical chores. The fifty-three-strong cast – including child actors and choirboys – were shepherded throughout with a smiling calm that would have won prizes at the Royal College of Nursing.

Rothenberg's was one of two teams which took charge of alternate productions in the Olivier. They had known they would be responsible for *Galileo* since the New Year, when they read the play and chatted tentatively about the difficulties it might present. The group comprised Rothenberg's deputy, Elizabeth Markham, who would eventually control the show in performance, and three assistant stage managers. Their jobs were rotated from show to show; one would 'prompt', annotating the moves and any script changes, and taking aside actors who kept getting the same lines wrong; another kept up the supply of rehearsal props, hustled the props department for the real thing, and informed them of the inevitable additions; and the third liaised between the rehearsal floor and the costume and wig department, so that actors could attend fittings – three or four *each* during the course of the production – without disruption to Dexter's work.

The candelabra (second model) is attended to by David Goodfellow

Rothenberg ensured that actors always knew their rehearsal calls, and took especial pains conveying new artistes round Lasdun's labyrinthine building. Actors who would not be in for a performance on a given evening and would not therefore see the call board were telephoned; those whom Rothenberg knew 'tended to go discoing at night', were politely asked to phone in themselves. The stage managers met at the end of each day to marshal the latest changes – new pieces of furniture, revised exits and entrances – and all such information, especially as it affected scene changes, was later tabulated by Rothenberg and distributed to other stage departments in advance of Week o. As often as not, the team would then have an evening performance to work on; it had fallen out that Rothenberg's crew were running two of the three other productions in the Olivier repertoire when the Brecht play opened.

During rehearsals for *Galileo*, James Boisseau was replaced as prompter by a former child actor called Neville Ware, following a two-week overlap period. Boisseau had become bored by the concentration on small areas of stage management work and reckoned the National was over-staffed. Having recently worked with much less proficient outfits, Ware welcomed the chance to do one job really well. In the four weeks up to and including that in which *Galileo* opened, Ware left the theatre before 10 p.m. only on seven occasions. He was seldom in later than 10 a.m., and was lucky to get an hour off at meal times.

Which scenes were to be rehearsed when was calculated mathematically by staff director Kenneth Mackintosh. Dexter would let him know the scenes he wanted to concentrate on over each week, and Mackintosh would divide the time available overall by the length of each scene. Scenes in *Galileo* tended to get about ten times their playing time for each rehearsal. Of course, there was more to it than this. All but four of the adults in the cast were already involved in other National productions. As well as matinées, these placed other demands on availability such as rehearsals to freshen up a play that had been out of the repertoire for a while, and those for changes of cast. Mackintosh was also in charge of understudy rehearsals for *Galileo*, which began during the fourth week of the rehearsals proper. There was an understudy for every role – some actors understudied parts smaller than their 'principal' role – and the idea was for the understudies to have the play learnt and re-hearsed by the time of the first public preview.

Accompanied by stacks of charts and plans, Mackintosh collaborated with Dexter when the principal cast was worked out, and he later drafted the understudy cast with Ann Robinson for the director's approval. With so many actors playing so many parts, it was no easy task to avoid casting somebody for a scene in which they already had a role, or close to a scene in which they figured prominently. Against his wishes, Mackintosh himself had been persuaded by Dexter to play a small part in *Galileo*; he would therefore find himself waiting to 'go on' when somebody would come up and say, 'Is it all right if I go to the dentist on Friday . . . ?'

A staff director was attached to each major production at the National and was much more than a cross between assistant director and stage manager. As a group under Mackintosh's captaincy, the staff directors were a permanent fixture in the theatre's hierarchy, a corporate *éminence grise* just below the top bracket. Like most of the management, they were housed on the fourth floor. Mackintosh had been a valued member of the company since the early 1960s – recruited by Dexter, as it happened – and his role in shaping the progress of actors and visiting directors could be vital. Each staff director did research in advance of a production, and kept an eye on the play in the director's stead after it had opened. He or she helped directors compose the programme cast lists – worrying over such questions as how characters would be described – and gave talks to visitors. During the dress rehearsal and preview stage, Mackintosh sat with Dexter in a viewing box at the back of the stalls and took anything between 70 and 110 notes each time the play was performed. These would then be delivered verbally to the actors or in memo form to other departments. Mackintosh's working day ran from roughly nine in the morning to eleven at night.

Mackintosh's group were in close touch with Michael Hallifax, as company administrator a key figure in the National's planning. Hallifax was formally in charge of the touring, casting, music and scripts departments, but his principal task was to make a workable timetable of the 22-week cycle and to relate this to the distribution of personnel. Daily schedules were worked out at least nine months in advance –

showing exactly what by way of rehearsals, change-overs, and performances would be going on in each auditorium; similar information in compressed form was distributed by means of 'quick reference' charts which, when *Galileo* was in rehearsal, already went up to June 1982. In six years, Hallifax had compiled 105 'quick references'. Adjustments to the repertoire could always be made, of course, but no later than nine or ten weeks ahead because of the publicity printing deadline. As well as the programme of the three theatres, Hallifax had to juggle productions on tour or being filmed; holidays; limits on the number of change-overs owing to the availability of stage staff; and the desirability of a production being given on different nights in successive weeks. There were occasional special arrangements, too: of his demanding roles in *Othello* and *Amadeus*, Paul Scofield would not give more than four performances a week, and he was guaranteed a break of two days between one play and another.

Among a miscellany of other jobs covered by Hallifax was the allocation of places in the dressing rooms: there were 147 places for a total of 160 actors and 40 musicians. Rooms accommodated one, two, or six actors; some had showers, some bathrooms and loos; some were nearer to one theatre than others. Hallifax had to decide who went where, taking due account of status and age. He had seen staff at the National mushrooming since joining in 1966, but had recently lost all three of his touring assistants as part of the cuts.

Nevertheless, Sir Denys Lasdun claimed that twice the number of people were now working in the South Bank building than he had been led to expect when designing it.

Chapter Eight

Toughening

During the second week of rehearsals, Dexter worked with a vengeance on the ideas he had come up with after the run-through. He heightened emotions and sharpened conflicts. He pushed Brenner and Gambon into a more aggressive relationship, and dwelt on the latter's sensual delight in food and learning. He demanded humour: 'Don't play it like *Private Lives* but be aware of the farts and grunts as well as the truth.' He jumped on vocal fuzziness and sent Gordon Gardner in hot pursuit of assorted individuals. Among them was Michael Thomas, whose performance Dexter had found 'a touch sentimental': he prescribed bringing the voice down half an octave to 'toughen up' the older Andrea.

Week 6, Thursday

The voice coach was charged with improving an abusive chant set up against the imagined witch by the young boys in the final scene. This work was conducted during a snatched ten minutes in the busy corridor outside the rehearsal room. The three lads looked distinctly sheepish as Gardner, in impeccable tones, urged them to relish the taunting words with rhythm and venom. 'Including the naughty word,' he said. 'I'm sure you're not allowed to say it at home.' The boys sang out:

Mary Mary sat in a mess
In her little pinky dress
Got the dress all stuck with shit. . . .

They repeated the chant with increasing enthusiasm and, while intrigued actors from other productions passed by, the little trio did their best to relish the word 'shit'.

The border scene was almost obsessing Dexter. One evening in the previous week, Herbert had read the dialogue over to him while he tried to envisage the blocking. One of his ideas involved nearly the whole cast forming a queue of people hoping to cross the border. He kept repositioning the various elements around the circular playing area – frontier post, would-be emigrants, customs desk, 'witch's' house.

A jug of milk was especially problematical. In the course of the scene, Andrea buys milk from a guard and places it on the old woman's doorstep. One of the boys then calls out that the Devil has conjured the jug from nowhere. Dexter acknowledged the importance of superstition in the scene, but his task was to stage it without embarrassment. How come the boy had not seen Andrea fetch the jug? Long before, Dexter and Brenton had decided that milk was a crucial image in the play, and Brenton believed that – if Brecht had worked more on this scene – he would somehow have linked the milk with the books carried by Andrea. In the opening scene Dexter had the young Andrea wipe a dribble of milk from Galileo's glass and swallow it. Now his older self did the same with the jug. But there were precious few lines to cover this and other 'business'. Half-way through the afternoon, the director said: 'Howard's going to have to write some more if he wants the scene. To hell with the estate. There's something missing, and even then I'm not sure it's right.'

But he pressed on, calling for more actors, ascribing roles in the queue to them almost before they had set foot inside the door, rearranging them, dissolving and creating 'families' and other relationships at the drop of a hat. He stopped and started over and over, reordering lines and eventually interpolating some of his own. The rejigged scene was transcribed at the end of the afternoon for presentation to Brenton. *A Short Sharp Shock* had just opened at the Theatre Royal, Stratford East, and Dexter was anxious about how Brenton would take being asked to rewrite 'rewrites' composed by somebody else during his absence. Also, he was concerned that the author's socialist sensibilities might be offended by a possible resemblance between the grim, hustling border scene he had been whipping up that afternoon and Checkpoint Charlie. But Dexter had the bit between his teeth and was now determined to retain the frontier sequence.

In rehearsal: a
rare moment of
tension between
Gambon and
Dexter

Week 6, Friday

The director had promised the company a run-through at the end of every week but called off that planned for today. He had been working in minute detail on short stretches of the play, but neglected passages would not have 'come on' since the first run. Dexter thought this might depress the cast, so no run took place. Nobody seemed to mind.

Week 5, Tuesday

Rehearsing the ball scene, Dexter's mood was almost beatific. He watched the actors enraptured, mouthing the dialogue to himself, eyes alert to every nuance of performance. Gambon did a funny, bum-scratching entrance and Dexter responded playfully. The actor was experimenting all the time with Galileo's physical aspect – trying a stoop here, thickening the voice there – and employing 'takes' and silent film comedy business. It was sometimes difficult to know how serious he was, but he never gave up. Basil Henson appeared in a dressing gown and Mark Dignam wore an old cape to rehearse as cardinals; Dexter urged on them the 'reasonableness' of the Church, just as he stressed Galileo's 'unreasonableness'. Stephen Moore seemed less at home than most. To him, Dexter suggested the use of a lower vocal register, and the performance became cooler, less expansive. The director kept on at Elliott Cooper, pressing him to 'fill out' his performance and avoid looking at the floor. 'Keep that pretty little nose in the air,' he instructed.

Cooper had thought Lodovico should harden over the course of the play but it seemed the boss wanted him tougher from the beginning. There were times during the afternoon, Cooper said, when he wished Dexter would lay off him a bit, but he was getting nothing like the pressure applied to the two boys in *As You Like It*. On that show, Cooper himself had been something of a butt: having come bouncing back then might even have helped him get his present job. But just as he needed to manage his relationship with the director, so he had to nurse his role, and not be seduced by banter away from serious work. This was how he had observed 'even the most entertaining of the senior

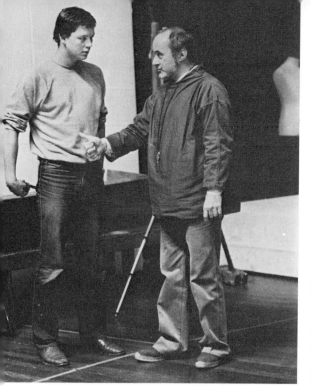

Tough words for
Elliott Cooper (left)
from Dexter

Mistakenly, Galileo's
disciples greet the new
age. *Left to right:*
Michael Thomas,
James Hayes, and
Simon Callow

actors' conducting themselves. Only now, felt Cooper, had something in the air about his rise from the ranks begun to dissipate. Anyway, the atmosphere was definitely better than it had been on the Shakespeare.

Week 5, Wednesday

Dexter worked strenuously at 'roughening' Michael Thomas, to good effect. Several actors declared that it had been a first-rate day and reiterated their appreciation of Dexter's approach. He cut out the small talk and got on with the acting. But the director was still unhappy with the smaller-part players. He had recently seen the Royal Shakespeare Company in *Nicholas Nickleby*. Their acting was of a much more even standard, he said.

Concurring with Dexter, Hall later pointed out that a solution to the National's technical problems would enable more plays to be put in the repertoire, and more work for all would create more incentive.

Week 5, Friday

Quite a party of spectators squeezed on to the viewing platform for the second run-through, giving it the feeling of a first night in plain clothes. They were not disappointed. Gambon was beginning to take command, trying out even more comic techniques and bold gestures. His scenes with Andrew Cruickshank acquired the proportions of a roaring melodrama; Galileo's address to the young Prince Cosimo before his illustrious courtiers was played with devilish slyness, tongue irresistibly in cheek; and when blindness and senility begin to hinder Galileo, he kept the character just this side of being an old buffoon. (Selina Cadell worried about the laughs Gambon raised in rehearsal in case they discouraged him from experimenting.) The actor's words had a resonance, and – at this stage – a slightly posh, enunciated quality that emerged incongruously from the small mouth in his rather bedraggled face. He used this to great effect in the comedy, but there was also a sense of distance between actor and character – of alienation, in fact – that would have gladdened Brecht's heart. What remained to be seen was whether he would complete the building of the performance on time, or whether it would remain – as it now seemed – interesting but in places rather odd.

There were electric moments. The welcome spontaneity of Cosimo's combative confrontation with the boy Andrea unfortunately went so far as to make the young actors forget their lines. Eisler's penetrating music and Peter Land's accomplished delivery made the carnival ballad – heard now by most of the assembled for the first time – perhaps the most sustained piece of theatre in the afternoon. And later in the play, when Galileo's pupils are briefly misled into thinking he has resisted the Inquisition, the new age really did seem to have dawned. Individual performances, too, were being coloured in: Basil Henson had abandoned some of his poise, offering a sense of the little man inside the Pope; and Simon Callow managed to utter a page-long set-piece speech as if he had not thought of a word of it beforehand. A visual pattern for the final scene had been settled on at last, and a subdued Dexter later reaffirmed his belief that the sequence would work. But he would not be drawn into predictions, telling the cast that the run 'was a sort of step forward'. He complained, however, that 'some people with about ten lines are still screwing them up' and asked them all to come in quicker on cue. Marc Brenner afterwards received a wigging for gabbling.

This was the rehearsal after which people started daring to think the show might be something special – it might not even be very successful, but it would be special. And Kenneth Mackintosh was elated at how much had been achieved in three weeks. 'John does *direct*, doesn't he? He gets on.'

As things turned out, it was as well that he did.

Chapter Nine

Dressing up

One person who refused to believe *Galileo* would be anything other than a disaster was Ivan Alderman, the costume supervisor and a great friend of Dexter's. It would, he promised, have a certain magic at first, but after Dexter's departure the play would reassert itself and turn the production into a flop. 'I loathe and hate *Galileo*,' he rasped. 'It's what I call left-wing intelligentsia.' Alderman was a short, slight man with piercing eyes and a rather harsh tongue. His department was, everyone would say, a law unto itself; or rather, a law unto Alderman. Here a little patch of theatre as it is supposed to be had sprouted among Lasdun's sobering concrete; here you were allowed to burst into tears, run screaming up the fire escape and otherwise dramatise yourself. In the office, with its pot plants, ample cocktail cabinet and delightful homoerotic pinboard, Dexter sought refuge after rehearsals. Andy Phillips used to kip down in a recess a little way along the corridor, so this part of the fourth floor became something of an outpost for Dexter's people.

Alderman had a remarkable tale to tell. His father gambled, and his adored mother was continually rushing him off to escape from the bailiffs; one night, he remembers, they were obliged to sleep on the floor of a bakery. But a façade of bourgeois gentility was kept up as he was ordered to 'look warm!' and lie to his schoolmates about the poor diet they were living on. His only ambition – never fulfilled – was to be a trapeze artist, but during the war he managed to find some solace in the comradeship of the fire service. Having served his apprenticeship as a tailor – 'my boss gave me twenty-five shillings a week, though he said I should be paying him; and that's how I think it should be today!' – he went into costume making out of desperation, and hated the job. He continued to hate it, but at the same time managed to build up some of the finest theatre wardrobes in the world – at Stratford-upon-Avon, its namesake in Canada, at Chichester and then at the National. He would stay in Stratford, Ontario, for only six months each year, smuggling his earnings back home in cash; when investigators quizzed him, he would claim to have earned the money showing tourists the 'pornographic' spots of London. The joy was that he could live off the money for the rest of the year without having to pick up a pair of scissors.

During one of his sojourns in Ontario, a young Canadian of Icelandic origin walked into the wardrobe and rather apologetically asked for work: the first job he did convinced Alderman that the boy was a genius, and suggested a way out of the costume making he himself loathed. He and Stephen Skaptason have worked together ever since, Skaptason cutting, Alderman overseeing. The Canadian was the physical opposite of his colleague – large, round, shy, softly spoken – and had a huge reputation among the *cognoscenti* as a costume cutter. He had a passion for every kind of costume, including, he said, dog blankets, and only excepting hooped crinolines because 'they always look like a joke.' Until this pair's pioneering work, costumes dated pre-1800 were tailored according to post-1800 ideas; they reasserted the more authentic methods and combined them with innovations in the use of felt to produce costumes that look like clothes rather than costumes.

A store of 11,000 garments had been built up at the National, two-thirds of which Skaptason cut. He had an encyclopedic memory and could say where the fabric came from on a costume made fifteen years ago.

The department's low-ceilinged work rooms were clustered together on the fourth and fifth floors, serviced by an especially wide lift to carry the racks of costumes. With the dressing-room quadrangle on one side, and outside terraces on the other, they occupied one of the few parts of the building where daylight came from more than one direction. The work benches and stools were high, surrounded by wobbly piles of fabric and drifts of cigarette smoke. Despite the histrionics occasionally brought on by pressure, the atmosphere was of fierce – almost monastic – concentration, the rattle of the machines sweetened by the constant murmur of advice from Skaptason to his underlings. As chief cutter, he specialised in female clothes; he and the 'male' cutter each had three assistants, augmented by specialists and casual help. It was a cutter's job to understand not just the costume drawings but the approach being taken to the character, too. He then advised the designer on fabrics and how they might behave when made up, and studied with her reams of samples gathered by the department's buyers.

The cutting itself was the most crucial stage in a costume's life, after which the cutter supervised the assembly of the garment. Skaptason determined the stitching that would be employed, pointed out inconsistencies in the hang of material barely perceptible to the untutored eye, and answered such queries as what sort of thread to use for the tie at a collar and how it should hang when in place. Most fabrics were dyed before being made up, and painted afterwards; later still, they were usually 'broken down' – that is, made to look used or worn.

In the National's costume department, Jocelyn Herbert was always welcome. She reciprocated their perfectionism and was a stickler for research. Alderman appreciated her 'high-bred' taste, though even he was heard to mutter about the time she took to reach final decisions.

Among the freelance experts brought in was Gaelle Allen. As milliner for *Galileo*, she was charged with reflecting the idio-syncratic shapes of the early seventeenth century without making hats that looked unnaturally stiff. Not satisfied with existing techniques, she developed a number of prototypes especially for the show. For the Venetian senators, she devised a way of using conventional hat blocks upside down; for the Doge, she piled clay onto another block, making sure Herbert approved the precise mould of the point at the back of the hat. Felt would be cut flat and steamed on to blocks to make the body of each hat; alternatively, costume material was bonded on to a calico shape. Herbert and Allen worked together on the elaborate decoration of the Doge's headgear, referring to an engraving from a slightly earlier epoch, and employing relief embroidery. The result looked like the genuine article perfectly preserved. It also illustrated the care taken over costume at this level. The Doge was an important but small role, and the scene concerned lasted at most five minutes. The hat took a week-and-a-half to make.

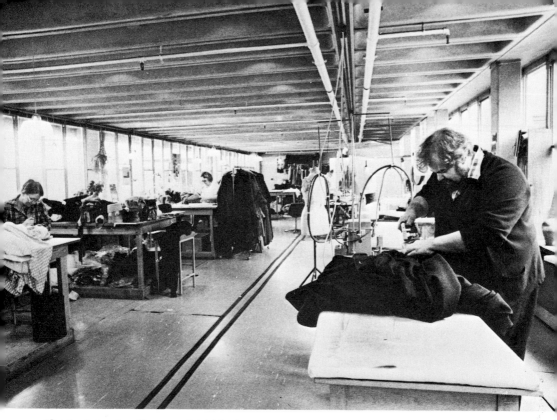

'Cutting': Stephen Skaptason (*right*) in the costume department

Freelance milliner Gaelle Allen

But profligacy was not admired, least of all by Alderman's redoubtable lieutenant, Cynthia Goodall. She co-ordinated the costume fittings, as well as looking after gear that was usually purchased outside: shoes, tights and – a 'nightmare area' – gloves. For the Pope's young acolytes, she had shoes bought in an Oxford Street sale, then painted; the young Cosimo's gloves were a ladies' pair from a similar source. Tights she imported from Germany at £5 a pair, instead of a British-made and less resilient variety that would have cost £8. But even the tights were carefully ordered, and arrived in bags labelled with the actors' names: 'Herr Cooper', 'Herr Sleigh', etc. Goodall guarded certain codes. Soles should never show brighter than the shoe, for example, but black rubber soles might mark the stage floor. 'Chrome' – a kind of suede – was best for soles; but the ball-scene shoes had come heeled with leather instead of rubber as requested, so these had had to be 'fluffed' or scratched to improve their grip.

A novelty on *Galileo* was that the scene shifters were to wear white boiler suits. On starting work at the National, stage personnel were issued with all-black outfits (and protective shoes required by law). But Dexter and Herbert, committed to making things manifest, had decided against discreet clothes for the scene shifters and small number of actors' dressers who would be on stage in the course of scene changes. Goodall therefore had to collect the measurements of about thirty extra people. White boiler suits were then purchased, and dyed to a different shade of white that would match the floor of the disc. The suits came direct from the factory; matching socks from Marks and Spencer; and plimsolls from all over the place. At the same time, Goodall was keeping records of the measurements of every actor in the company, including an outline of their shoe shape and in some cases even ophthalmic prescriptions. She also collected, magpie-fashion, accessories that were increasingly difficult to come by, and would often send someone off to a street market to forage. Her room contained drawers full of spectacles, watches-and-chains and wing collars, racks of shirts, and cupboards, boxes and skips full of shoes. And this was only one territory in Alderman's domain.

On the fifth floor, in a tiny skylit room which they liked for its 'studio' feel, sat Michael Jessop and Daphne Lord. They

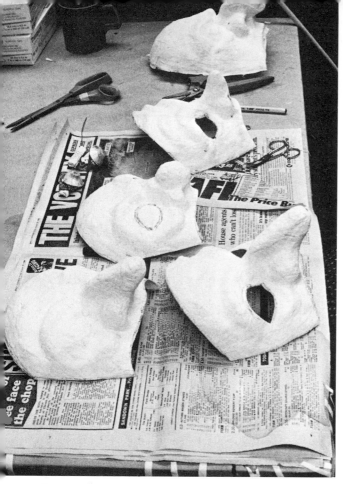

Bases for *commedia
dell'arte* masks to
appear in the ball scene

Michael Jessop with
one of the masks
nearing completion

made up the costume accessories department. He was a trim, affable West Yorkshireman who had been with the National for five years, and she – brought in specially to help with *Galileo* – had been head scenic painter at Sadler's Wells as long ago as the mid-1940s. Their tasks included making a dozen striking *commedia dell' arte* style masks for guests at the ball; seven sets of ladies' jewellery; fifteen dignitaries' Orders and chains of office; and assorted clasps, ecclesiastical rings, and neck chains. In addition, Jessop constructed a crown for the Pope, a three-tiered affair with pearls and jewels; to these he added ornaments specially cast from a mould he had made of a furniture trimming. Unlike most of the masks, the crown was based on a drawing, but Herbert saw it after several days' work and asked for something more sober. Jessop then set out on a new, starker model made in felt with gold braid that would be shellacked and painted to give the effect of marble sculpture. But something from the furniture shop – in this case, keyhole covers – would still appear on His Holiness's head. Each crown took several days.

The great size of the masks worn by the carnival crowd made their shoes look excessively dainty, whereas the impression being sought was of grossness. Jessop was therefore asked at short notice to produce some larger footwear, and over one weekend knocked up eighteen pairs of felt boots; the next weekend he draped them with hessian, painted them, and 'broke them down'. Despite the extra time put in, he was not planning to see a performance of *Galileo*. He explained with a smile that, although he loved being among theatre people, he preferred the cinema for a night out. 'Besides, they only give you one free ticket. What use is one ticket?'

Someone whose disenchantment went deeper was Joyce Beagarie, in charge of wigs. Once in a while, she liked to get away from the National and work in commercial theatres where the characters were more up-market. 'Here you spend an awful lot of time breaking down the best to look the worst, and kicking peasants' wigs around the floor. We do a lot of peasants in these art houses.' Alderman confirmed that their stock of garments was particularly strong on paupers' wear. There must be some significance in the fact that film and television studios clamour to borrow rags from the National Theatre!

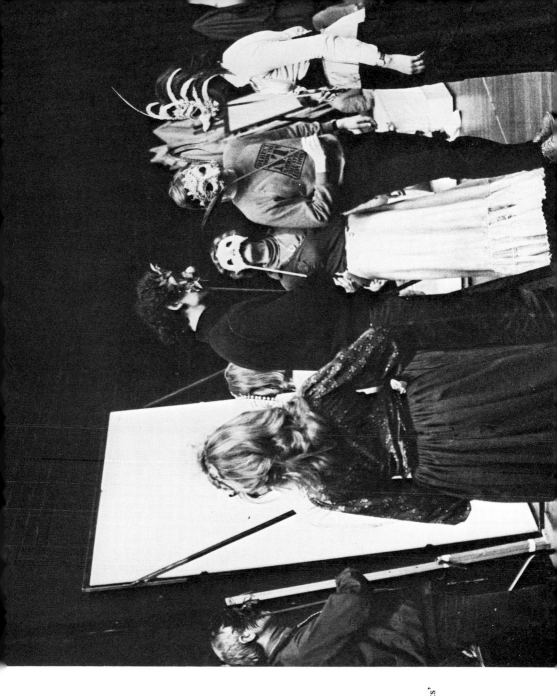

In rehearsal: masked 'guests' at the ball chatter

Beagarie's was one of the few teams to stay abreast of schedule on *Galileo* – but only by going ahead on certain work without Herbert's say-so. She and her five assistants – each of whom had City and Guilds certificates in hairdressing and wig making – were busy with 29 beards and moustaches, 6 tonsures, and 13 wigs, including 3 wigs and 3 beards for Gambon alone. Each wig took between 18 and 30 hours to make and needed between 3 and 4 ounces of hair. Painstakingly the hair was drawn through the lace with an action similar to that used in rug making. Most of it was human and came ready-dyed from the supplier, although yak was occasionally used for silvery facial hair. Poland, Yugoslavia and Italy were the biggest sources. The National's own (Polish) supplier asked from £5.50 per ounce for the cheapest to £8 for long blonde hair.

The preponderance of beards made this show unpopular. Each beard had to be cleaned and re-curled after use; one person would need to spend a day on beard maintenance after each performance. Also, making a beard look natural is almost impossible, because growth attached under the neck – where beards sprout in real life – would constrict the actor's throat. Beards made in sections were less constricting, but experience had demonstrated that little portions of beard went missing easily on large-cast shows.

The tonsures came in two models: most involved a small piece attached to the actor's own newly cropped hair; for Simon Callow, however, they were obliged to supply the alternative of a complete wig with tonsure, as he wanted to preserve his own long hair for his role as a 'drop-out' in Alan Ayckbourn's comedy *Sisterly Feelings*.

False noses were another speciality of Beagarie's but she refused to make the balladeer's as bulbous as requested. She thought that Herbert was underestimating how large the nose would look on stage, and felt some of the real nose should be left uncovered to vibrate as the actor sang. The actor was asked to run through a few bars wearing a couple of old noses to establish this point precisely, and he provided a cast of his own nose on which the false one could be built. False noses were a perishable commodity. On application, the very edge was melted down to blend with the real skin, and a similar operation took place afterwards, so that a whole layer of the nose was lost

Costume fitting: Audrey Price (back to camera) and Jocelyn Herbert
fit Brian Kent with a 'Brueghelesque' mask and rags from the
National's copious collection for the carnival riot

at each performance. Beagarie's team opted to make three noses initially, but knew that if the balladeer perspired a lot this would speed up the hardening process and require them to make more.

The shape of an actor's head – as affected by a false nose or wig – and the colour of hair could, Skaptason said, affect the whole balance of a costume; and the same garment could look radically different on two different people.

Fittings were therefore an acid test, and people from all areas of the costume department would attend. For a good quarter-of-an-hour, each of the three Cardinals was required to stand under the spotlight in one of the small fitting rooms, while a press of people flitted about, held things up against them, and discussed them as objects.

Stephen Moore was unrecognisably severe in dark wig and beard, spectacles, and full crimson outfit. Suddenly, the image that he and Dexter had dreamed up of the Inquisitor as an ascetic, youngish man made sense.

Had more modern dress been involved, the actor might have had more to say, but on this occasion the conversation was led by Alderman and Herbert. Moore was asked to parade up and down, kneeling several times to ascertain the best length for his skirts. Other questions that engrossed the assembled were what sort of ring would be worn; where the Cardinal's cross would hang (determined by where across his front the actor liked to fold his hands); and what colour gloves should be used. Red leather was settled on for the latter, but Alderman was anxious that they might not be made in time. When Mark Dignam subsequently tried out his robes as Cardinal Bellarmin, a protracted debate started up as to the most appropriate buttons. Several different sizes were tried. Alderman asked if they would buy buttons and dye them or have them specially made, and warned that they should be mounted on black, not silver, for fear of catching the light. This particular fitting lasted well over an hour. When Basil Henson used his ball mask with the robes Alderman tentatively suggested that this ensemble might get laughs. 'It doesn't matter,' said Herbert. 'Really?' said the costumier, raising an eyebrow and returning to one of his favourite themes. 'Is one allowed to laugh at *Brecht*?'

Ivan Alderman's department produced 147 costumes for *Galileo*. Of these, 79 were new, 68 came from stock but were altered considerably and worn only by 'minor characters'. By another hiccup in the theatre's planning, some key staff were on holiday at the time, so 15 of the new costumes had to be commissioned from outside. Approximately 71 pairs of tights were used, all but 9 of which were bought specially. A total of 36 pairs of plimsolls were worn, as were 25 new pairs of shoes and 64 pairs adapted from stock. Cynthia Goodall estimated that there were 170 full costume fittings, but could not put a figure on the separate sessions for hats, shoes and wigs.

Chapter Ten

Pressure

Week 4, Monday

Because of a bloodshot eye, Dexter rehearsed wearing dark spectacles. On this as on several previous mornings, he began by asking a member of the cast to read out a Brecht poem. All one needed to know about Brecht was in the poetry, he said. Brueghel reproductions were then passed round, and Dexter asked those who were not wearing masks in the carnival to devise their make-up from the paintings. He choreographed for the crowd a gradual, threatening movement in from the edges of the playing area, climaxing in an explosive procession round a tall, Maypole-like model of Galileo. He told Peter Land that his rendering of the ballad was 'too Drury Lane', asking Gardner to work with the actor on flattening out the vowels. Land's last job had not, in fact, been far from Drury Lane: he had played Freddie in the revival of *My Fair Lady* at the Adelphi, and drew some attention to himself by marrying the show's choreographer, Gillian Lynne. Singing the one song in *Galileo* and taking a couple of mute roles might have seemed like demotion after a West End lead, but Land had wanted to join a classical company. He was delighted to be at the National, except that they were pressuring him to understudy, which he didn't fancy.

Among the onlookers in the gallery were an actor called Robert Oates and Timothy Norton's father. Every child performer had to be chaperoned, and both Norton and Brenner were usually accompanied by their fathers. Norton senior seemed quite unimpressed by the growling, foot stamping, yelping and cheering that Dexter was strenuously orchestrating. As was his wont, he spent the morning reading the

Harrow Observer. Robert Oates was in fact a member of the cast, although a TV commitment had kept him from joining rehearsals until the end of the first week. He had auditioned for Land's part, but had been asked to understudy Gambon and play The Speaker. In this role he called out the number of, and a brief synopsis for, each scene. Oates sat through every rehearsal simply in order to give these announcements. This morning, he did not say a word until 12.55. Nevertheless, he was one of Dexter's most fervent admirers.

In the afternoon, Dexter smartened up the 'Pope dressing' scene. So intricately did the bowing, incense-waving, genuflecting and costume-portering depend on each other that it always took a long time to trace the cause of accidents: if someone arrived somewhere late, it was usually as a result of something somebody else had done wrong several minutes earlier. It was striking how vigorously the actors participated in the process. Far from waiting to be told things, they were constantly offering ideas and self-criticism. Nobody objected when the director asked that, although they were wearing long robes, everyone should rise and kneel on the same knee. Elliott Cooper, having been to a Roman Catholic school, acted as an unofficial religious adviser for this scene and was rewarded by Dexter with the nickname 'Sister Veronica' for his pains.

While the dressing is in progress, the Cardinal Inquisitor pressures the new Pope to let the recently arrested Galileo be tortured. Dexter worked on marrying the Inquisitor's movements with the ceremonial. At one point, he was pulling Stephen Moore around by his arm while gesticulating frantically at a couple of the acolytes. Moore had meanwhile forgotten his lines and was waving his free hand at Neville Ware for a prompt. He and Dexter looked like an agitated octopus, while the others crept demurely around.

Week 4, Tuesday

Dexter failed to turn up for rehearsals. He was ill. Nothing to get alarmed about, stressed Kenneth Mackintosh. Having nursed his shingles, he had neglected an earlier problem: blood pressure. This had returned – hence the eye trouble yesterday –

and Dexter had decided to rest for the day. He had sent instructions for that day's work and would be back tomorrow.

Mackintosh rehearsed some of the earlier scenes, each at full whack first and then down at conversational level. The atmosphere was eerily hushed, as if the actors felt a little lost. After scene one, Mackintosh asked Cruickshank how he'd felt and Cruickshank said he'd felt fine and asked Gambon how he'd felt and Gambon said fine, except that the blocking was getting a bit bunched in one place. When this had been sorted out, everyone felt fine. It was very quiet, though.

In the morning the floor of the carpentry shop had been cleared for delivery of the truck from Kemp's. After a minor problem with the colour-coding, the bits of the truck were assembled, and its 100 feet of track laid down in sections. Originally, Herbert had thought the truck would travel up a ramp and on to the disc. But Malone and Kemp's had designed a track for it that would remain on the floor of the existing stage and beneath the disc. The wheels were attached to thin, upright panels supporting the platform. When the truck reached the disc, the panels slid through narrow slits in the disc and carried the platform just over its surface. That morning they found that the truck moved along its rails and did so silently. It remained to be seen whether or not it would jam when it met the disc.

Week 4, Wednesday

Eric Dunn had less luck. The hoops for the armillery sphere were at last delivered. Driving round the front of the theatre, however, the driver passed under a low arch which struck the largest of the hoops, severely denting it. This had to be returned to the works, while the others lay idly round Dunn's shop.

Contrary to Mackintosh's forecast, Dexter didn't come in.

Week 4, Friday

He did not, in fact, come back all week. Rehearsals went ahead, building to the run at the end of the week. Consolidation was

Week 4, Tuesday in the carpentry shop: a section of the truck is lowered on to its rails

The wheels are attached to thin panels which support the main body of the truck

achieved, and Mackintosh was able to get the understudy rehearsals well and truly under way. But the electricity, the sense of being driven, had dissolved; people stayed cheerful, though Gambon was heard to mutter that not having Dexter was 'terrifying'. For Michael Thomas, the absence was particularly frustrating. After the drubbing of the previous week, he felt he had begun to make strides, for all Gardner believed he had lost power in the third run-through. Now Thomas said: 'The director is someone you put things to, a kind of sounding board. Without him you tend to go in on yourself and that's negative.'

The script requires a small daughter for the balladeer and his wife. For some time, Ann Robinson thought – and hoped – that Dexter had forgotten this additional performer. But in time he had asked for her, and five-year-old Michelle Middleton had been recruited. Earlier in the week, on first encountering the carnival crowd in full growl, Michelle became upset and was carried out in tears. It looked as if she might drop out of the show altogether. But she was keen to act, and her mother explained to her that such bizarre spectacles were part and parcel of theatre life. Then Ann Robinson spent time showing her some of the other work that was going on in the building.

A break was called at today's run, and the carnival sequence was taken gently for Michelle to get used to it again before it was done at full pelt. Everyone held their breath. There was no repetition of the scene: Michelle was back with them. Meanwhile, Marc Brenner was achieving the increased stroppiness Dexter had asked for and Elliott Cooper was developing a fine swagger.

The director's absence had its compensations. Now people could smoke in Rehearsal Room 2. Dexter had once run Gambon into the corridor when he tried to take a crafty drag. As he did so, the actor joked: 'It's like school here!'

Everything would be all right, as long as Dexter was back on Monday.

Week 3, Monday

Dexter returned, pale but busy. He confirmed that the trouble had been blood pressure not a recurrence of shingles. In the

The complete truck – without floor boards – on its rails

morning, he worked on the first scene, and was delighted with the growing 'realness' of the characters. He read a little lecture about the difference between speed and pace. Speed meant simply going too fast, and risked confusing the audience. Pace meant keeping something happening all the time without gaps for breath or recovery. Olivier had a method of taking a breath, not between sentences, but just before the end of a sentence, thus eliminating a pause in the dramatic action where a full stop occurred in the text. They would do well to emulate him. Dexter reiterated this in the afternoon, when he came to 'the most difficult scene'.

At the request of the Florentine court, the Papal Astronomer examines Galileo's findings with the telescope. For monks and scholars of the time, the mere fact that Galileo is being taken seriously is outrageous enough. When, at the climax of the scene outside the Collegium Romanum, Galileo's ideas are confirmed, the bottom falls out of their world. While awaiting the verdict an assortment of clerics and astronomers complain to each other – and to Galileo, who sits apart quietly – about the threat they see looming. Their beliefs now seem absurdly fundamentalist, but this needs to be presented without a hint of caricature. English performers are strong on subtlety, irony and charm, but not so hot – unfortunately in this case – on simple power. Here the actors – many of whom came to the scene after a quick change from a similarly supporting role – were expected to presage the end of the world as they knew it in brief speeches and as rounded individuals. It was enormously tempting to act as a featureless chorus.

No sooner had the scene started than Dexter jumped on Nigel Bellairs, playing a monk. His speech was only a sentence long, but the director asked for it again. 'As soon as you get a vocal problem,' accused Dexter, 'you start compensating with the hands and arms and the voice disappears.' The actor tried it again. 'You took four pauses. You can't take any.' He did the speech again. 'You're going too fast.'

After getting through the scene once, a grim Dexter sent Gambon off for a cup of tea and gathered the others around him. 'The reason why Gambon is so far ahead of you is not just that it's a bigger part. It's that he's not afraid to colour the text without getting poetical.' They had to be interesting, he added,

Michelle
Middleton in
rehearsal

but at the moment were failing. Actors of their generation might not think they needed techniques such as Olivier's breathing device, 'but you'd better learn some before you do this play.' They resumed the scene without Gambon and Dexter drilled them. Speeches, sentences, even phrases were pounced on and taken over and over. The director was abrasive and clearly unhappy. 'Please, please, please, do not be afraid of every syllable of every word.' He was soon asking for feats of breathing the actors clearly didn't feel were possible. 'Jump cues if you have to . . . bite on the text . . . use your vowels . . . clatter your teeth around the words.' And don't, he stressed, try to solve the scene emotionally. The problem was one of technique.

'Stop everything,' cried Dexter, scampering over to Roger Gartland, who played the leading astronomer. 'Until you can sit still and deliver the lines you're nowhere.' As Gartland repeated his speech, Dexter held his shoulders and kept easing them back, trying to relax them, rolling the actor's head and urging: 'Don't play hunched, don't play aged.'

Dexter was back all right. But his full spleen was reserved for young Adam Norton, playing the Thin Monk. One of many ways Norton caused displeasure was to forget a recently in- serted move, as he marched threateningly toward Galileo. 'You've been screaming and bleating for four weeks and now you've forgotten the move. Vocally, that was terrible.' Dexter slumped in his chair, muttering to the voice coach 'Gordon, tell him something.' For once, the director seemed speechless.

Quietly, Gardner offered: 'It's fanaticism, isn't it?' and this appeared to revive Dexter. 'That's it!' he called out to Norton. 'Do you know what a fanatic is? You're looking at one, dear. You're reducing me to Tony Guthrie. Give me a performance and I'll give you a note. Try to give me something some time this week.' Later he sat the actor down for a conference with Gardner, stressing the intensity and heat underlying the speech. After several more attempts, he said: 'Adam, good. Well, I mean . . . if we'd had that three weeks ago I might have felt better.' The actors were dazed but still co-operative. The scene was by now more seriously passionate and any trace of caricature had certainly vanished.

Afterwards, Dexter explained how his patience was ex-

Week 3, Monday: a troubled rehearsal of the scene outside the
Collegium Romanum

Collegium rehearsal: Dexter instructs Roger Gartland. At the
benches (*left to right*) Glenn Williams, Peter Needham, Robert
Howard, Peter Land, Gartland and Dexter

hausted by actors who failed to 'bring things' to rehearsal. 'Norton and Gartland seem incapable of responding to reason. They've got smashing parts, and they've not come on in three or four weeks. I'm pouncing because I'm tired of asking.'

In the canteen, Adam Norton said he had wished the ground would open and swallow him up. 'I felt "Forget it, I don't need the aggravation, I'll go off and be a bank clerk".' It was not that Dexter was wrong about the scene. 'I know what he wants, I'll give it to him, and Dexter knows that.' But he resented the manner of the director's asking. A number of the older actors said they felt Norton had been unreasonably singled out. Perhaps more disturbing was that Norton related Dexter's dissatisfaction to the director's psyche rather than to his aesthetics.

Norton was a well-spoken lad who had been to public school and Oxford. This got up Dexter's nose, he thought. And there had been an element of reassertion by the director after his week's absence. The actor had, funnily enough, forecast to his wife before leaving for work that there would be some kind of scene that day. Ironically, he had not wanted to be in the play in the first place. It was only as a jest that he had suggested to Kenneth Mackintosh he might play the Thin Monk, and if it hadn't been for his mortgage he would have moved on from the National some time ago.

The gap between actor and director was partly a generational one. Dexter called Norton 'boy' just as he had been called 'boy' by George Devine. This sort of authoritarianism was part of his culture. For all the humanism of their repertoire, the Royal Court in the 1950s and early 1960s was a place where you did as you were told. During a lighter moment in the rehearsal, Dexter told someone: 'Donald Wolfit would be proud of you.' When mention of the old actor-manager drew a laugh, Dexter added defensively: 'I don't care, Donald knew his job.'

That afternoon's dramas raised other questions of approach. Dexter believed in meticulously worked-out blocking and repeated run-throughs. Some of the actors might have preferred less runs, but they only had praise and gratitude for the blocking approach. It was such a relief to know, so to speak, where you stood. If an actor ran into difficulty, Dexter's solution was proffered in terms of moves and a technical 'breaking up' of speeches. He did not use improvisation, and, although he had said

Collegium rehearsal: Adam Norton (book in hand, playing the
Thin Monk) berates Michael Gambon (in the foreground, Galileo).
Also in the picture (*left to right*) Nigel Bellairs, Peter Dawson,
Melvyn Bedford, and Artro Morris

Collegium rehearsal: Dexter berates Adam Norton (left) at a brief
conference with Gordon Gardner (nearest camera)

that he might, he never sat the actors down to scrutinise the ideas in the play. Brenton remarked that he would have been more disturbed by the omission had not the production served the play so patently well. He had opted to let Dexter 'do a number on it'.

Many younger – and not so young – performers like to ask hard questions about their characters' motivation and backgrounds. This is a welcome antidote to the waffly, generalised work that goes on in so many pockets of our theatre. A different director on *Galileo* might have gone in for that sort of talk, and perhaps used improvisation to explore the lives of the characters away from the text; this could have helped fill out the smaller performances. Dexter would contend that such delving was not his responsibility, though it is doubtful whether it can ever be pursued effectively in isolation from the ensemble.

Interestingly, Simon Callow enjoyed Dexter's approach, despite a strong Stanislavskian background. Dexter was a trainer, he said, not a teacher; and a lot of actors' talk about improvisation was 'indulgence'. Dexter's relentless attachment to technique was, however, to take its toll on Callow later.

From Dexter's point of view, the task was to get a difficult play on in a difficult theatre with a mostly young cast; it needed to be audible, clear and lively. That was a very high priority, and, whatever the cost, it was one that Dexter would not funk.

But he was haunted by his image as a director strong on ensemble work and choreography. Behind this were bitterly resented implications that he was less adept at intimate emotion and things intellectual. Selina Cadell endorsed his self-assessment, wishing actors in the larger-canvas scenes could have seen him at work on the more domestic sequences. Of the carnival, Dexter talked almost contemptuously: 'It's easy, traffic cop stuff. Any director can do that.' Perhaps there was some sour satisfaction when a number of critics saw in that passage his only directorial lapse.

Week 3, Tuesday

Eric Dunn had been looking at the hoops for the armillery sphere. One of them was too big, and he would have to ask for it to be remade. There was now only a fortnight before the scheduled erection on stage of the finished sphere. Meanwhile, pressures from shows other than *Galileo* were mounting on the metal workshop and all departments. Bill Bryden's pageant-like production of *The Passion*, with its street floats and illuminated trade union banners, would shortly be travelling to the Edinburgh Festival before coming to rest at the Cottesloe. *Watch On The Rhine* and *The Provok'd Wife* (both initially to be seen out of London) would be dress rehearsing on successive days in the Lyttelton, and *Line 'Em* – for which Dunn was building the set – would be starting at the Cottesloe, all three within days of *Galileo*'s opening.

Members of the props team responded to such situations with versatility and buckets of elbow grease. To cover the huge grassy mound on which the family entanglements of *Sisterly Feelings* were played out, the entire department had spent a fortnight doing nothing but unpick string and knot it on to a hessian base. Richard Pocock, one of the most active on *Galileo*, had an especially good eye for putting things to unexpected uses. He had bought a toy for his cat, a ball on the end of a very springy wire. The cat had destroyed the instrument at once, despite the fact that it came from Harrods. But in the middle of the night, Pocock realised that another of these gadgets would make a suitable accessory for the balladeer, combining the ideas of the 'Fool's bladder' and revolving earth. Then models of astronomical systems were required for Galileo's household. For the earth in the Ptolemaic, they used an old brass door knob, and paper with a stained wood pattern covered the plywood with which the spheres were made. This week, too, they received an urgent request from Dexter for 'dressing' for the study scenes, miscellaneous items that were not expressly demanded by the script but would enhance the 'feel' of the set for actors as well as the audience. Quickly they pulled together a collection of books – thin volumes, as all books were in Galileo's time – compasses, an hour glass, and documents that looked remarkably authentic but were in fact made from photocopies. One of the department's special skills was 'breaking down' or 'distressing' props. Vinegar was applied to make leather look older, and cheese graters were used if bleach did not do the trick on fabrics. To walk about the truck set for Galileo's study and littered with 'dressing' really was like stepping back in time.

Week 3, Thursday

There had not been a hint of 'off' acting from Yvonne Bryceland since the first week. On the other hand, she had not appeared to take flight with the revised characterisation Dexter had elicited. Suddenly, rehearsing a speech in which Mrs Sarti attacks Galileo for ruining his daughter's marriage, she released a tirade of extraordinarily articulate power. Everything clicked into place. From then on this was always one of the production's most magnetic moments, and Brenton said that it helped reveal between Galileo and the housekeeper a quasi-marriage not discernible on first reading the text.

Dexter had been putting increasing pressure on the actors, forcing them to heighten every line of every speech. Disagreements became quarrels and quarrels became rows; smiles became giggles and giggles became laughs. By now, the cast were readying themselves for costume by wearing practice skirts and odd capes, and most of them knew their lines.

In one passage, however, the pupils became hopelessly confused as Galileo tried to disprove Aristotelian ideas about floating bodies with ice, needle, paper and a bowl of water. They ended up describing the opposite of what their teacher was supposed to be showing, thereby 'proving' Aristotle right. This lapse perturbed Dexter less than did Elliott Cooper's contribution. Rejecting Virginia when her father resumes his heretical researches, Lodovico consistently lacked the 'weight' the director sought. Over and over, he urged the actor not to 'apologise' for his lines. The character was now 'a dangerous landowner, a bully, no longer a juvenile'. Despite some progress, Dexter remained disgruntled and spoke coolly to Cooper throughout the rehearsal.

Dexter's temper was similar, in fact, to that in which he had started the week. But this morning was enlivened by the camp talk at which he excelled. He liked to make a fuss about haircuts some of the men would require. Stretching back in his chair with an unashamedly gleeful smile, he said of Michael Thomas

The Collegium scene in performance

In performance: Yvonne Bryceland (as Mrs Sarti) lets fly her tirade at the seated Gambon (left). Meanwhile, Elliott Cooper (centre, as Lodovico) prepares to leave, deserting Virginia because her father has taken up his heretical researches

and Marc Brenner: 'Both those little darlings are going to be like shorn lambs. They don't call me Delilah Dexter for nothing.'

Later in the day, there was more harassment for Cooper. A mask class had been set up, which became a rehearsal of the ball scene, although this had not been officially 'called'. Cooper was one of three actors asked to take up a mask from a table and extemporise. Results were not being sought, they were told, and the actor did not come up with much. This seemed to frustrate Dexter, and the company were surprised by how quickly the session was curtailed. Dexter said later that he had been amazed by how few of them had experience with masks. The actors felt he had been unhappy because, untypically, he was not sure of what he was looking for; but this observation failed to alleviate Cooper's growing discomfort.

In highlighting the element of 'apology' in his performance, the actor felt Dexter had 'put his finger on my weakest point'. He was pursued by a feeling that he could be found out at any moment, and this prevented the relaxation necessary to unleash the brute force required. Dexter had begun rehearsals with aggressive friendliness, but had recently been sharply critical. 'You've got to be better,' he had said. 'It's no good going behind a shell every time you walk on stage.' Cooper knew exactly what Dexter meant but was not sure his way of saying it was helpful. He had begun to ask himself if he was experienced enough for the role and was losing that confidence Gordon Whiting considered so important. Cooper summarised: 'Dexter has woken me up in the middle of a nightmare and told me what I'm dreaming.'

Week 3, Friday

Shortly after lunch, word went round the props workshop that Sir Peter Hall – not a familiar figure in their part of the building – would be dropping in for tea around 3 o'clock. Beakers were scrubbed in a flurry and modest light refreshments bought in. The supremo did not arrive as scheduled, but by around four he had settled down to find out how things were going. When he asked if anyone had any comments, Richard Pocock answered simply: 'Help!'

A lighter moment in the tense mask class

Mask class: Dexter invites Elliott Cooper to contemplate his
masked self in the mirror

Meanwhile, Dexter was watching the regular run-through. For most of it he sat slumped in the gallery, his head down like a bull about to charge. During the 'Pope dressing' sequence, however, he leapt up, and gesticulated furiously at Stephen Moore. The actor's moves had gone awry; neither was he very sure of his lines. As Dexter sat down again, he threw his eyes to the ceiling in an expression of despair.

Afterwards, he sought out Gambon for praise and then said: 'The rest of you – soggy!' On Monday they would be working on stage in the Olivier, he reminded them.

'We'll see if that knocks some of the sogginess out of you. And if that doesn't I will. Some of you are playing small parts as if they were small parts. If that's your attitude you'll stay playing them for the rest of your life.'

I did not like to ask Andrew Cruickshank, who had first appeared on the London stage in 1930, what he made of that.

There had been more stick for Adam Norton that day, and increasing harassment for another younger actor called Michael Fenner. Fenner played a guard in the frontier scene, and the hectoring speed with which he kept the emigrants moving was crucial to Dexter's conception. The actor was sturdily built, but his voice had a husky 'young' quality that the director disliked. After the run, he told Fenner: 'I'm getting Sunday School acting from the boys but I don't want it from you. I don't like replacing people but I might have to.'

Departing for the weekend with these words ringing in his ears, Fenner was at a loss. He had had sessions with Gardner, who had encouraged the use of a downward inflexion. The actor felt this was 'voice' acting, and, against Gardner's judgment, had forecast Dexter would hate it. Fenner was proved right, and this made him wonder how much co-ordination went on between coach and director. In fact, before taking individual sessions, Gardner made a point of getting Dexter to commit himself as to what he was after. But rehearsals themselves were supposed to be experimental. Dexter was not the first director to ask for something, get it, and dislike it, or ask for one thing, get something else, and like that. Nevertheless, several actors felt the value of the private voice work lay less in innovations

Week 3, Friday: Stephen Moore (foreground) in the 'Pope dressing' scene during the run-through at which he appeared to upset Dexter

Another who displeased: Michael Fenner (holding staff) as the frontier guard. On the left is Michael Thomas (the older Andrea) and crouching at the trunk is Marc Brenner (here playing Giuseppe)

made than in the opportunity granted to polish what existed away from Dexter's beady eye.

Disaffection was growing. There was dark talk among a number of the cast about retaliation if Dexter started 'biting people'. Gordon Whiting remarked that outsiders thought all theatre directors were martinets, but Dexter was unique in his experience. 'Even Guthrie was light, but with Dexter there's a bit of venom.' He added that, on the other hand, actors working at the National ought to be able to take it.

Exacerbating these problems was the impossibility of getting close to Dexter as a person. In New York, Jocelyn Herbert had campaigned to get him to attend first-night parties, without success; and he had described himself as a social disaster. James Hayes recalled missing a morning's work when his son was ill, and later being summoned by the director. To his astonishment, Dexter proceeded to enquire after the boy. Hayes said: 'Much better . . .' but did not get another word out before Dexter said 'Good,' and changed the subject. Hayes's own respect for him remained intact, but he was not sure he would feel the same if Dexter had taken a dislike to him.

Week 3, Saturday

Around the cocktail hour the new workshops manager John Malone was to be found in the Green Room, drinking alone and feeling isolated. His family were still up in the North of England, and he was fed up with getting the cold shoulder from National personnel whenever he suggested a new approach.

Two incidents were typical. The false shutter was to comprise several hardboard sections which it was Yves Rassou's task to give the appearance of metal. Rassou felt they should be covered with metal foil then painted; Malone argued for spray painting the boards directly. Rassou resented the second method as it would involve stencilling thousands of tiny holes onto the boards: these were intended to enhance the metallic effect but would only be visible at close range. Malone said Mark Taylor had suggested the stencilling, but Rassou held Malone responsible. Relations were not eased when Herbert saw samples of both and opted for Rassou's. Naturally, the painter wished he had been left alone to pursue his method in the first place.

The truck floor produced yet more strife. Originally, the plan had been for plywood boards to be painted to look like rows of planks, but Herbert said she would prefer the genuine article and asked for nine-inch-wide scaffolding boards. Malone told her that there would not be time to obtain and fireproof boards of that width, adding that he had in stock some six-inch boards that could be used. Herbert acquiesced, and Malone congratulated himself on a useful saving: these boards had been bought to make the rehearsal room stage that had later been abandoned. At this time, Peter Hartwell was absent on a teaching assignment. Herbert mentioned what had happened on his return, and said she would have much preferred the wider boards. Hartwell reckoned that it would not be necessary to fireproof the boards she wanted precisely because of their extra thickness. He set off for the carpenters' shop and persuaded John Phillips of his point of view. By now, however, the truck was almost completely covered. Malone said later that replacing the thinner boards had wasted £1,000 worth of materials and four men's labour for a week. Further, although he was seen as the villain of the piece, he claimed that somebody in the production office had given him the mistaken information about fireproofing in the first place.

He had started out at the National with an easy-going style. Unhelpful responses, he maintained, had forced him into what had been described as running the workshops like a factory. He felt as bad about this as anyone else.

In these circumstances, the only surprise was that – as he propped up the Green Room bar – John Malone stuck to halves.

Chapter Eleven

On stage and off

Week 2, Monday

Despite Dexter's earlier demands, this turned out to be the company's sole rehearsal in the Olivier before Week 0, the production week. Their own playing areas were marked out on the *Othello* stage, with a segment missing. Odd people slipped in and out of the auditorium, but without a proper audience it was about as welcoming as an aircraft hangar. The arcs of purple seats, widening relentlessly as they receded from the stage, made a mouth that threatened to swallow up all the actors' energy. Understandably, Gardner concentrated in the warm-up on 'throwing' sound up to the back of the circle. Dexter was animated and tense. He kept moving into different parts of the theatre, urging actors to sit at the extreme sides of the auditorium when not on stage to get a sense of the vocal task. Once, he stood rapt in attention with his back to the stage. At other times, he would stop people smoking and ask casual visitors to go away.

The cast gave a resilient account of themselves. They had gone in to the day's work determined to show a 'huge effort', Selina Cadell said, and if this was not quite apparent it only proved the Olivier's capacity to soak up performances. Some of the blocking – especially in the truck scenes – looked cramped, but Dexter's main concern was that actors were only now appreciating the reality of what he had told them about voice. Gambon seemed comfortable, although he considered that it had not been until his third production there that he had begun to get the measure of the auditorium. He and Dexter came as close as they ever did to falling out when the actor wandered way off the playing area in an early sequence. When he asked with typically unabashed innocence where the scene ought to be played, Dexter retorted: 'You know that perfectly well. You're just trying to get attention.' Marc Brenner was shouted at for making an entrance from the wrong place, and received more attention than most in the matter of vocal level. His first scene with Galileo was taken over again, but for the most part Dexter seemed happy with the rehearsal. After a long duologue between Galileo and the Little Monk who leaves the Church to work with him, Dexter pointed out that it was perfectly possible to stage a conversation in the Olivier. What was necessary was not excessive volume but keeping vowels and consonants clear and 'every syllable energised'.

At the end of the afternoon, Michael Thomas had come away crying that he hated the Olivier. Another actor had a more nagging anxiety. Stephen Moore said he feared he might not 'get' the 'Pope dressing' scene. The crux of his concern was that two distinct things – the dressing ritual and his argument with the Pope – were going on simultaneously. The audience were to be asked the equivalent of the old co-ordination exercise in which one hand describes a circle across the front of the tummy while the other pats the head. With all that was going on else-where, Moore found it difficult to trust that he was not 'droning on and being a bore'.

Week 2, Tuesday

While the actors were trying out the auditorium, the disc floor had been installed in Rehearsal Room 2. Mark Taylor confessed that the job had been done 'in a hurry' and this morning Dexter complained that it was uneven. Over lunch, it had to be re-laid. Taylor and colleagues had bigger headaches than this, however.

Gratified as they were that the expected 'storm' had not materialised, they were still finding Dexter and Herbert too elusive for comfort. According to the director's existing plans, more scene shifters would be required than were on the books, but he was reluctant to discuss the matter further. The tran-sition out of the carnival was particularly bothersome, though Dexter had eased this a little the previous day by opting for a second interval following that sequence. Taylor's scepticism about Malone and the workshops persisted. The substructure for the disc remained unfinished. A metal chassis for the balustrade – which was to travel on the same rails as the truck – had not yet been made. The truck itself was still only half covered. Taylor had today received a 'very rough' sketch of the frontier barrier, and this was the first he had been told about scenery for the sequence concerned.

Malone, stage controller Andrew Killian and others of the production staff dropped in to Taylor's office and they all ruminated mournfully over their lot. Whispers suggested that *The Romans in Britain*, for which Brenton had been doing some last-minute rewrites, might not go ahead as planned. The show was already behind, but of course a substitute at this stage would only mean more problems for them.

There was some comfort, however, in that Taylor had at last found the required distortion for the back projection slides. After three attempts, tests that morning had proved his latest calculations accurate.

In the afternoon, Hall watched a run-through of *Galileo*. Word went round that he had been asleep for part of the time. As he later readily demonstrated, he had a way of screwing up his eyes while listening carefully to the text, and this had given the inaccurate impression he was dozing. In the contentious final scene, a new line was inserted without Michael Fenner being informed. This made the actor appear to 'dry', which he would have liked to have avoided in front of the theatre's chief.

Week 2, Wednesday

Arriving for work, Fenner was perturbed to see that a rehearsal of the border scene was called for that afternoon, when he would be appearing in a matinée of *Sisterly Feelings*. How could they work without him, unless the worst had happened? After the matinée, he met Kenneth Mackintosh in the corridor. The staff director asked if Fenner had received a message from him to go to the Casting Office. 'It's bad news, I'm afraid,' said Mackintosh. The actor had not had any message, but said 'Don't tell me, I know what it's about.' Shortly afterwards Gillian Diamond confirmed that he had been dropped from the part at

Dexter's request, and in the teeth of opposition from her. He had her assurance that the management's opinion of him was unaltered. Fenner explained to her that he was not hurt by the idea that he was too young for the role, but by the manner in which the affair had been handled. Why had Dexter not said more to him, for example? Later he told his agent that he felt like walking out of the show. The agent sympathised, but Fenner decided against. To have left would have made things exceedingly awkward for Glenn Williams, who had been given his role. Besides, there was the small matter of fees. Actors at the National were paid a basic wage plus so much for each performance given.

On top of the heartache, Fenner had lost his only speaking role in the play.

Week 2, Thursday

Fenner was called out of a rehearsal for *Amadeus*, and found Dexter waiting in the corridor. The director was friendly and apologetic. According to the actor, Dexter said that Fenner should not have been given the part in the first place, adding 'It's my fault, I'm sorry,' and patting his face. Dexter later claimed that Fenner had been treated with perfect propriety, having been given warning at the end of the previous week. Williams was neither a better nor worse actor than Fenner; it was made clear that the issue was suitability, not talent.

But there was a sting in the tail. Nobody had said to Fenner that he was expected to assume Williams's role as a non-speaking guard on the frontier, though it seemed likely that this was the case. Believing that a small demonstration of actors' rights was in order, Fenner sat on the sidelines when it came to the scene at this afternoon's run-through. From gestures sent in Mackintosh's direction by Dexter, it became evident that the actor's assumption had been correct. When he was at last asked to replace Williams, Fenner agreed.

Since Monday, Dexter's mood had been highly business-like. The play was now being run every afternoon, stage management and acting ensemble alike racing fleet-footedly to change over from scene to scene. Gambon's interpretation did not alter,

but the assurance with which he executed it grew all the time.
Selina Cadell had well and truly taken the 'plunge'. The professionalism of Marc Brenner's conduct continued to impress, and
Dexter refused to cosset him. The older Andrea's closing
speech is particularly addressed to a boy called Giuseppe, with
an implication that he will inherit the scholar's mantle. Having
played the younger Andrea, it seemed only appropriate that
Brenner should also take this role. In the very last moments of
the play, he would walk upstage after the departing Andrea and
examine the galaxy projected across the shutters. Yesterday,
Dexter had complained that Brenner ambled; today, that he
'acted' the walk too self-consciously. The more notes Dexter
gave him the better, said the boy, 'because I get a nice big shout
if I do things wrong.' And another of the youngsters, Stephen
Rooney, habitually matched the adults' application in the
difficult 'Pope dressing' scene. Even when, as frequently
happened, the Pope's stand-in crown wobbled at the climax of
the scene, the attendants remained expressionless. After the
run, Dexter said quietly, 'Thank you. It's coming along nicely.'

The armillery sphere was not, unfortunately, and the
schedule had by now had to be adjusted. One of the circles was
still missing, and Eric Dunn decided he must chase up the
suppliers again. Meanwhile, his workshop was increasingly
cluttered, as work continued on the sprawling substructure.
Not counting the ramps, they already estimated that 2,500 feet
of steel would be used. Dunn remained unruffled.

Week 2, Friday

Dexter missed rehearsals again. In the morning, the company
were told that he had been locked in his flat and was waiting for
the police to let him out. He was duly released in time to take a
scheduled lunch with Arts Minister Norman St John Stevas, but
it turned out that he had to return to the flat afterwards to deal
with the locksmith. As a result, he did not come to the theatre
all day. People asked themselves how he had contrived to get
locked *inside*. A light-hearted air of mystery was heightened by
newspaper reports that the body of a murdered lady violinist had
been found at the Met.

Simon Callow took the opportunity of the director's absence to try out a Belfast accent. For some time he had felt at sea and unsatisfied by Dexter's 'technical' answers. He reckoned he always needed a distinctive character into which to transform himself. 'I find it very hard to play simply good people,' he said. 'If the Little Monk were a paraplegic with designs to blow up the Vatican I'd be fine.' He had tried to get a physical sensation of the character by wearing rough garb and sandals but this had not helped. Then he asked himself whom he knew that the monk resembled, and thought of an Irish friend. He acknowledged the risk that people would think he was making an explicit but unintended political comment; but the accent gave him something to latch on to and he decided to keep it in for Dexter's return. The truth was he was finding *Galileo* a much less gratifying experience than *As You Like It*.

Gambon looked forward to the final week of rehearsals with some trepidation. Because of a preponderance of performances of *Sisterly Feelings*, in which he appeared, he would be working every evening but one as well as rehearsing during the day. The actor joked that, had he been a 'ponce' like Olivier or Paul Scofield he would have made sure in advance of a light workload. The management had not bothered to protect him because they thought of him as 'sweaty and smelly and working class'. As it happened, Scofield was indirectly involved in the scheduling pile-up. Michael Hallifax had hoped to avoid playing the Ayckbourn at the end of the week, but Scofield had asked for a break around then and this was the only available play that did not involve him. Scofield was, Hallifax explained, 'very tired'.

Everyone who has ever worked in production management dreams of a show that will evade last-minute crises and emergency work into the early hours. Stage personnel are expected to perform eleventh-hour miracles as necessary because 'the show must go on'. Officially this is never taken account of in planning, but there is a suspicion that the artistes who run theatres presume on their technicians' dedication more readily than they admit. Of course, at the dress rehearsal stage actors and directors drive themselves too, but the practical set-up prevents their putting in the same hours as their 'non-artistic' colleagues.

Simon Callow
and Michael
Gambon
rehearse the
Little Monk
scene

At the National, strong unions and high overtime costs have encouraged the institution of an 11 p.m. deadline; the notorious 'all-nighters' are a thing of the past. This makes for less romance, but it also reduces the exploitation and self-exploitation that remain prevalent in our theatre. The National attempts to plan ahead in a way that is unusually painstaking – bureaucratic, even – but is only appropriate to the scale of its operation. People sometimes say of opera houses and large theatres: 'How awful that their aesthetic endeavours should be trammelled by rules and regulations.' But the performing arts have yet to make a case for their exemption from the struggle for decent hours and conditions of work. In this sense – and despite the fact that John Rothenberg said he would not recruit someone who asked a lot about hours at a job interview – the shop stewards and management at the National should be seen as progressive, not conservative.

Week 1, Tuesday

In an attempt to ease the *Galileo* production week, some of the necessary work on stage was scheduled to be sneaked in ahead, during change-overs between other shows. Today the grand black arches of *Amadeus* were due to be dismantled and replaced by the bumpy green hillock for *Sisterly Feelings*. In the process, the accident-prone armillery sphere would not be putting in an appearance as had been hoped, but the plan remained to position the 'Rome door'. In performance, this portal would be lowered from and raised to the flies; the task now was to get it up there ready.

Before that, however, the newly printed slides were to be tested. The projection platform had been in place since the end of Week 5, but the distortion had been ascertained with a prototype. Now to be seen for the first time were the actual slides that would be used, projected with the equipment and from the position as in performance. Bill Bundy, Jocelyn Herbert and a number of heads of stage departments sat chatting fitfully in the stalls during an inordinate delay. They pretended not to be nervous – the mathematics had been got right, and mathematics were reliable, weren't they? – but the atmosphere was edgy. The wait became so strung out it seemed it must portend disaster. At last the slide that would open the show was thrown on to a temporary screen. It looked well-nigh perfect. A couple more were tried. No fault could be found. Slide upon slide came up for scrutiny: the definition and proportions were fine. Bill Bundy – a man not given to optimistic proclamations – agreed with Jocelyn Herbert: 'We're on our way!'

The 'Rome door', magnificent even as it lurked in the shadows of the wings, was now carried to lie prone centre stage. About fifteen men and the lone woman member of the master carpenter's crew handled it with robust expertise. The head of this stage department was incongruously named, as he did not actually do much carpentry, and his people preferred 'stage technicians' to the more prosaic title 'scene shifters'. They were a motley assembly whose loud good humour belied their sensitivity to the artistic temperament: Dexter was a great favourite of theirs, for example.

Their task appeared straightforward: to tie the portal to a bar that had been flown down, then raise it above the stage. But so much scenery from other shows was crammed in the flies – 'baroque Italian lumber' Dexter called it – that a tight squeeze was certain. Almost immediately there was a hitch.

Much of the *Amadeus* scenery had been stored away in the crowded area behind the stage, but a gauze screen remained in the flies. This had ladder-like attachments, normally connected to another scenic piece, which jutted out at a downstage angle and now appeared to be catching on the bar intended for the portal. They were removed by men climbing up on alarmingly spindly mobile platforms, called 'Tallescopes', but these efforts failed to solve the problem. The portal was raised upright by the crew, like a corpse being put back on its feet, and Doug and Alan Sutton were summoned to attach the doors themselves and do other fine-tuning carpentry. Every time the portal was raised to the flies, however, it moved smoothly to begin with then shuddered and came to a halt, remaining in view of the stalls. Mark Taylor decided it must be catching against the gauze, which was itself hanging at a very slight angle.

Meanwhile, chunks of the *Sisterly Feelings* set were being put in place at the foot of the stage for that evening's performance; this gave the portal the appearance of being buried beneath a green mound. As the flying experts continued to make nice adjustments to the gauze and portal, odd people wandered around, looking much less purposeful than they had at the beginning of the morning. Someone played 'As Time Goes By' on a piano in the wings.

The *Amadeus* gauze was now back down on the stage along with the 'Rome door'. Word went round that they were ready to go up again. The portal was being operated manually, the gauze screen on the notorious electronic system. They were raised together, slowly at first, then accelerating furiously. The portal at last seemed to be moving up higher and out of sight. Suddenly there was a fearsome thud and it stopped, swaying in an ominous manner over the heads of the stage technicians. Dust and chips of plaster showered the stage, and bars of spotlights swayed and clattered noisily above. The portal was clearly not going to fit. Later, it was brought down and taken away.

Taylor and others went into a huddle over this and sundry pressing problems. The 'Rome door' would have to be flown from a different position, but it could not be all that different as the portal must keep to roughly the same place on stage. More flying had been planned for Friday's change-over. Things were 'panicky' confessed Taylor. John Malone had left the building abruptly the previous Friday when his wife had suffered a suspected miscarriage. Bill Bundy meanwhile called a conclave to find out just how far behind the workshops were falling. At that meeting, Taylor learned for the first time that some important welding work on the disc's substructure would have to be done *in situ*. This and the delay with the portal meant that the fit-up, which they had been trying to keep as tight as possible, was already threatening to extend; it might after all be necessary to work Sunday. The chassis for the balustrade had now been farmed out to Kemp's and jobs on later shows were being commissioned outside. In his absence, Malone was the object of no slight vituperation. His colleagues were still bothered by rumours about the possible fate of *The Romans in Britain*. 'Well if we go ahead and build the set,' said Taylor as they broke for lunch, 'that'll make their decision for them.'

In Week 1 more time was spent rehearsing the border scene than any other. Dexter revised the characterisation of some of the emigrants, asking pointed questions, and ascribing them new life-histories and increasingly desperate situations. One family carrying its grandfather was told that it did not know if the old man would last until they got over the frontier. Foot-stamping, visa-waving, drunken carousing and responses to the action were minutely orchestrated, but 'generalised rhubarb' was ruled out. Everything was timed and 'set'.

The boys were marshalled as strenuously as the rest. As the scene picked up pace, so the youngsters were more tempted to gabble, and their chant directed at the 'witch' was still creating problems.. Dexter came down hard on any slurring of words.

Tiny segments of dialogue, one or two sentences long, were run over repeatedly; because of the numbers of actors involved, and the multitudinous pockets of activity, this was like launching and re-launching a ship.

Especially later in the week, though, Dexter seemed expansive and more relaxed. There was some agreeable light relief. He rebuked young Adam Stafford for being 'refined': 'I don't know where you go at night, but if it's Tramps stay out of there till the show's over.' Stafford then played the same speech in an accent several degrees broader than Eliza Doolittle, and Dexter roared with laughter, more fulsomely than at any other time. And for the outsider there were extraordinary sights, like that of the director – in deadly earnest – arranging the exact angle of Stafford's backside for a moment when he is kicked by the frontier guard. Dexter had plenty to be pleased with. Strengthening the Giuseppe–Andrea axis, Marc Brenner would now open a chest carried by Andrea and take out a book. While things continued hectically everywhere else on stage, the boy would examine the book with caressing, sensual fascination. It was a brief but unforgettable moment.

In the more domestic scenes, Dexter exploited a host of techniques to get things going faster and clearer simultaneously. One speech would break in to interrupt the preceding speech, for example, though this was not necessarily indicated in the text. In addition, the rewards of his fanaticism for blocking were increasingly manifest. In a later scene, a former pupil of Galileo seeks an audience to explain his apparent renunciation of the new ideas; he bursts into the house, approaches the scientist, is rejected and departs crestfallen. As it was played by

Michael Beint and choreographed by Dexter, the character's brief appearance traced a simple but telling circle over the floor of the truck.

Freer now of the rigours of *A Short Sharp Shock*, and the rabid press coverage it had attracted, Howard Brenton watched a number of these rehearsals. Far from worrying about Checkpoint Charlie, he said that the frontier scene reminded him of Istanbul Airport, where he had suffered an unpleasant encounter with the authorities. While work on this continued on the Wednesday of Week 1, Gambon spent the whole morning at a costume fitting. Next day, the canteen made a gallant gesture in the direction of wholefood principles and offered 'brown rice, jam and custard'. Giving this particular dish a miss, Simon Callow reported of the latest run-through: 'I dropped my accent and it's all going much better.'

For one member of the company, by contrast, things were going decidedly worse. A combination of domestic problems and the demands of his role as The Speaker meant that Robert Oates had failed to learn Galileo's lines. After a deal of subdued agonising, it was agreed that he be replaced as understudy to Michael Gambon. An actor called Peter Welch was recruited on the condition that he would know the part by the time of the first preview – now not much more than a week away. The management treated Oates gently. It was said that he would resume understudying in the autumn, and he was given a role in *The Romans in Britain*.

The fact that he had never lapsed like this before failed to cheer the actor. He had begun work on the production in high optimism. Now his admired Dexter was throwing out cryptic comments on The Speaker that he found hard to interpret, and he for his part had let the director down over the understudying.

Week 1, Friday

Standing on the Olivier stage and peering up into the black-slatted galleries of the fly tower was like finding oneself in a futuristic cathedral. The overwhelming size of the place became most apparent when – as during today's change-over from

Othello to *Sisterly Feelings* – the scenery was swiftly cleared and the stage left bare. Suddenly the stage rather than the seating was seen to occupy the greatest expanse of space.

Heavy rostra that made up the stage for *Othello* were carted away like so many cardboard boxes. The electricians – a stage department under the imperturbable Peter Radmore – busied themselves with lamps lowered from the flies and wheeled around on giant trolleys. Everywhere there were patches of fast but unfrenzied activity. Every one of the thirty or forty people now teeming on to the stage created a powerful impression of knowing exactly what she or he was doing.

A new position had been found for the 'Rome door', but the portal remained tucked away while Head Flyman Lennie Thomas sawed down its counterweight bar to avoid catching on yet more scenery from other shows. Another group prepared the 'rain bag' for *Sisterly Feelings*. This was a short, perforated screen folded back into a U-shape, strung across the width of the stage and loaded with rice. When a rain storm occurred to bring the first act of the Ayckbourn to an abrupt halt, the bag would be shaken, releasing a thin film of cereal to which appropriate lighting gave the appearance of rain. The odd unexpected shower was an occupational hazard for Olivier stage staff.

Today's contribution to *Galileo* was to be the assembly and positioning above the stage of the back projection screen and the aluminium framework. When the screen – a huge grey square, the sections of which had been specially heat-welded together in Germany – was wheeled on to the side of the stage, more than one person exclaimed that it was far too big. Not in the sense that it had been made wrongly, but rather that Herbert had miscalculated. Would not the slides overwhelm the dramatic activity they were supposed to be enhancing?

Three lengths of the framework were quickly assembled into an arch, then suspended above the stage. A second arch, having been put together at the back of the stage, was carried forward and placed beneath it. The first was brought slowly down, its feet intended to fit over two pairs of tiny prongs in the top of the lower arch. But one of the feet was jamming. John Mogford from Kemp's, who had helped build the framework, was sent up on a 'Tallescope' to investigate. He filed teeth-tinglingly inside the foot of the upper arch but it still would not fit. Then a

Week 1, Friday: The
Othello rostra are
carried off; in the rear
stage can be seen
sections of the mound
for *Sisterly Feelings*

The screen for *Galileo*
arrives

The central metal shutter has now been lowered, and the screen lent against it. The first arch of the aluminium framework is assembled, prior to being 'flown'

The first arch having been flown, the second is raised into position

John Mogford (left) and partner ascend the 'Tallescopes'

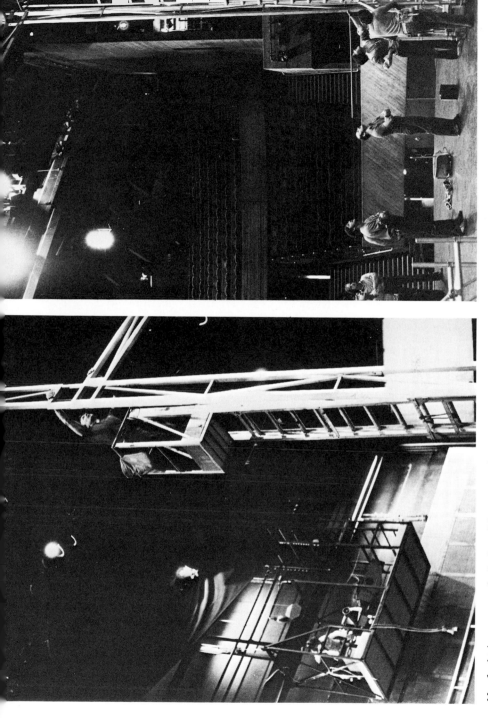

Mogford tries to persuade the feet of the upper arch to ease down over the prongs . . .

. . . observed by (*from left*) Mark Taylor, Rob Barnard (from the sound department), Roy Bernard (deputy master carpenter) and Rodger Hulley

block of wood was taken up to him and he hammered through it against the structure. The troublesome piece edged reluctantly half-way down but would go no further. There was more filing and head scratching. Then Mogford and a National man at the other side of the arch started hammering in noisy concert. At last the arch slid into place. This hold-up lasted over twenty minutes. Earlier the entire *Othello* set had been shifted in about an hour.

More perilous work was expected of the man from Kemp's when he had to feed into the very top of the structure the four cables that would carry the screen. A pulley block was flown down and a small orange 'bosun's chair' attached. Mogford sat in this keeping up a stream of jokes while the small group waiting with him went gradually quieter. A safety line was eventually threaded through the chair. Steadying himself against the side of the arch, Mogford was eased high up above the first arch and then higher still into the flies. Mark Taylor held the safety line; Rodger Hulley or deputy master carpenter Roy Bernard remained on the end of another cable attached to the chair. They kept their eyes fixed above, gently pulling at their ropes to help Mogford negotiate his way among odd hanging cables and bars of lighting. By the time he was at the top most other activity had frozen; his colleagues watched him like spectators at a circus, calling up the occasional hint or warning. Half-way through the job, the house lights were inexplicably switched out. When Mogford was finally lowered to the stage, dizzy but still smiling, there was an embarrassed silence where the applause might have been.

Because the National was a big place with a high turnover of work, no one production automatically dominated the corporate mentality. But escalating activity in the Olivier meant that here, at least, the birth of *Galileo* was making its presence felt. A piano was delivered to the musicians' box, and the choirboys – in plain clothes – explored the auditorium. The sound of music being rehearsed in the foyer filtered through, and with the heroic activity going on all over the stage, the cleaning staff were hard put to concentrate on dusting the stalls. Shortly before the end of the morning's work, the great slide screen itself was lifted toward the framework. Mark Taylor noticed that it had been left standing on a single small rostrum so that the

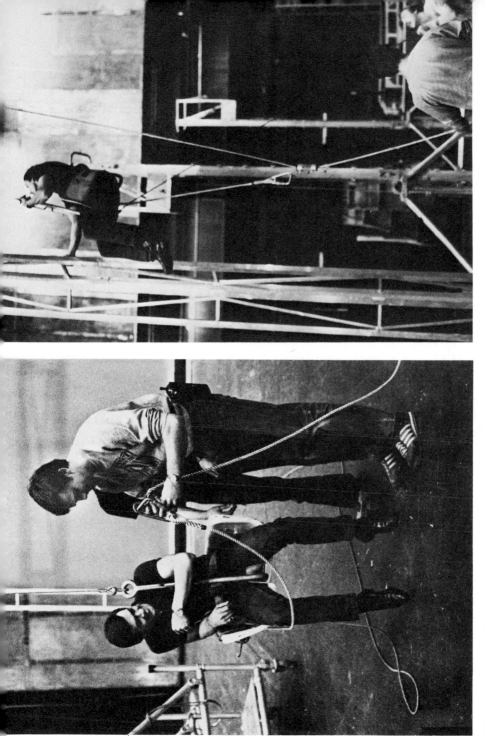

Week 1, Friday: John Mogford (seated, in the 'bosun's chair') keeps up the badinage as Roy Bernard secures the safety line

On the ascent, Mogford steadies himself

Mogford above
the first arch . . .

. . . and disappearing
into the flies

During this morning on stage, a second projector was flown up on to the specially built projection platform. Receiving it are Andy Torble (left) and Charles Bata

The first sections of the mound for *Sisterly Feelings* are positioned in readiness for that evening's performance . . .

. . . the job is almost complete

'Cracking' the penultimate scene (*left to right*) Selina Cadell
(Virginia), Michael Gambon (Galileo), Michael Thomas (Andrea as
a man) and Nigel Bellairs (as Galileo's ecclesiastical guard)

bottom strut had bent slightly. The screen was soon attached to the four cables and slotted into the framework, up and down which it would move in performance. The trim figure of Andy Torble, from the electrics team, had been in position on the projection platform most of the morning. Now he threw a slide on to the screen and an ironic cheer went up. The image was clear, but it was upside down.

A week from today, paying customers would be in for the first public preview.

After lunch, Dexter announced with an enormous grin that he intended to enjoy that afternoon's run and he defied any of the actors to stop him.

The director was to fly to New York in the evening, and return on Wednesday. Understudy rehearsals would be continuing, with as many as nine scenes called on Monday. On Tuesday afternoon Kenneth Mackintosh would oversee a run-through proper. Those actors with time on their hands would probably find themselves whisked off to the wig department for a haircut.

John Rothenberg reminded the company in Rehearsal Room 2 that the choirboys – who had been practising separately up to now – were present. Hardly anyone had missed the half-dozen eight-, nine- and ten-year-olds, however, as they had virtually taken over the canteen and consumed £11.41 worth of lunch between them. It was a measure of the expanding power of the production that the boys watched silent and unfidgeting through to the very last scenes. They were especially rapt when Galileo's friend Sagredo warns him of the possible repercussions of his research. Asked where God is according to his latest thinking, the astronomer replies 'Within us – or nowhere!' The choir – which was to introduce this scene with the words 'January ten of sixteen ten/Galileo abolishes heaven' – came from St Elizabeth's Roman Catholic Church in Richmond. One of them explained subsequently that Brecht's work had failed to shake his faith. 'It's only a play, isn't it?' he said at the first-night party.

A greater sense of youthful bravado was now emanating from Gambon in the earlier scenes, and the encounter between him and Cruickshank – work on which had never been easy, despite the surface politeness – was great fun. But beneath the humour through which Gambon had approached them, the character's dilemmas were increasingly apparent. At the end of the scene where Lodovico walks out on Virginia and the news of the new Pope encourages Galileo to turn his study into a laboratory of the forbidden, Gambon prowled the stage like a hungry animal, hunched but eager, crying 'I must know, I must know!' There had been some doubt about these lines, but they had been transformed into a remarkable moment. Two minutes later, the actor was turning over the pages of sheet music for pianist Kevin Leeman during the balladeer's song.

Elliott Cooper's confidence seemed, if anything, a little precarious, but Yvonne Bryceland soared and the story throughout the cast was of more polish and more consistency. Afterwards, Dexter rapped the rail of the viewing platform and murmured 'Thank you. That will be all. See you on the platform. Thank you. Very good.' He had conducted his last rehearsal in Rehearsal Room 2.

Later, the director said he felt Gambon had solved two major problems at this run. He had finally found a way of sustaining each scene as a separate entity, kicking the habit of referring mentally to action past or to come. Secondly, the actor had 'nearly cracked' the long speech of self-denunciation delivered to Andrea near the end (which at least one member of the company felt was Brecht 'going too far'). Gambon himself believed he had begun to get on top of this speech while Dexter was away ill, when he had spoken it purely for meaning. Dexter judged that Gambon was now 'relating character to argument and both to clarity'.

Dexter left for New York in subdued good spirits. Herbert had meanwhile been ushered into the Olivier to examine her aluminium brain-child. Quite rightly, she said it looked 'super'.

Chapter Twelve

Lights, music and publicity

Among those for whom *Galileo* now loomed especially large were members of the stage departments. Whereas the workshops served all three theatres within the National, most stage departments served only one. The Olivier and the Lyttelton had similar teams, while there was a smaller, less compartmentalised set-up in the Cottesloe.

After the Saturday evening performance of *Sisterly Feelings*, the Olivier closed to the public to make way for the *Galileo* fit-up. John Rothenberg's stage managers now moved into a higher gear, and for all the stage departments the Brecht play became their prime preoccupation. The departments in addition to Rothenberg's were: stage technicians, led by the Master Carpenter; props under Johnny Pursey; Ric Green's sound team; and electricians under Peter Radmore.

Stage management continued to captain rehearsals, but in the days to come the shifting of set, furniture and so on was to be handed over under their supervision to various other of the stage departments. The closer the actual performance, the more responsibility devolved on Rothenberg's deputy, Elizabeth Markham. From her control box at the back of the stalls, she was able to address on a three-ring intercom system stage technicians; sound, music and other stage management personnel; and the electricians, who had their own box nearby. She could talk via headsets with an army of individuals: the lighting and sound operators; the flymen on each side of the stage; musical director Dominic Muldowney in the musicians' and choristers' box; the truck operator; shutter operator; and stage management colleagues at either side of the stage. Of the latter, Angela Bissett in the traditional 'prompt' corner would actually call actors; she occupied one of two tannoying points on stage.

Markham herself could tannoy out into the rest of the building and had a rarely used telephone. There were cue lights dotted about the stage, and another in the box opposite the musicians' where Robert Oates and Neville Ware sat. When a scene change was due, Markham would give a visual as well as verbal 'stand by' call to those concerned. The visual involved a flashing red light; the person being called pushed a button to steady the light and tell Markham the call was acknowledged; when it came to the cue itself, a second light indicated this. Because such a network of people was involved, it always took a long time to go back over a cue. Apart from the scenery and props that had to be 'set back', everyone concerned had to let Markham know they had repositioned themselves. This drew from Dexter a few caustic comments about the National's 'computer', but the truth was that the stage management did not use one.

During performances proper, John Rothenberg would 'float' around at stage level, watching in particular the progress of the scene-changes. A report on each and every performance was circulated to various of the theatre's high-ups.

From her box, Markham would tannoy announcements to encourage the public into the auditorium near the start of the show. She could not, however, commence until the front-of-house manager popped his head inside her box with the all-clear. Then she had to check with her colleagues at stage level that the actors for the first scene were standing by. Her first cue indicated the end of the 'pre-set' – the state the stage was in as the audience entered – and the beginning of the action.

During the early days of the fit-up, Rothenberg and the electrics team each had consoles in the auditorium with which they could communicate with colleagues in their boxes and elsewhere. After the official first performance, Markham would help compile the stage management's 'Bible' copy of the play, detailing every cue and every task they carried out.

Apart from humping it from workshops to rehearsal room, the master carpenter's team did not handle the set until it was ready to go on stage. Then they shifted the scenery but not the props that decorated it. An early headache for them sometimes arose from the fact that the Olivier was on the third floor. With the drum revolve not fully functioning, scenery could not travel on it from ground to third floor and had to go up by lift; occasionally, the scenery was in sections too big for the lift.

In addition to production meetings, master carpenter Dennis Nolan was supposed to get advance information as to what a show involved scenically from ground plans, but these were precisely the sort of thing that came late on *Galileo*. Nolan worked closely with Lennie Thomas, trying to preserve order in the fly tower which he described as resembling Cheddar Gorge. His own private code marked scenic pieces to aid their reassembly.

Dennis Nolan had spent ten years as an actor before going along as a casual labourer to the Old Vic in 1976, and had once played a police sergeant in a short-lived West End thriller. During the *Galileo* production week, he was on holiday, leaving his deputy Roy Bernard in charge. Bernard had given up a lucrative job as a *Daily Express* photographer to work in theatre. Like Nolan, he started humbly, but he never regretted the change and particularly enjoyed working with Dexter. It was interesting that, however much expertise they had accrued over the years, few of these backstage people started out with a technical training. Many had begun in stage management, however. Sound manager Ric Green said 'Stage management teaches you about theatre etiquette, which is very important. Without it, you'll wear hard shoes on the set or bring fish and chips into the theatre.'

On the surface, *Galileo* was not a great challenge to Green's department. There was just one sound cue: the bell rung to herald Galileo's recantation. But there remained the question of whether to use electronic 'enhancement' for the choir – which Dexter argued forcefully against – and the more general problem of sound in the Olivier.

Acoustics had been the subject of some bad publicity early in the theatre's life, and as a result Green felt people went in expecting not to be able to hear. They then failed to make the sort of audial adjustment demanded by most big theatres, and would duly complain. Such objections were taken very seriously. The seat numbers of complainants were noted and sound reception for that seat was reproduced electronically on a simulated laboratory model of the auditorium. Since the theatre opened, additional acoustic absorption had been installed and Sir Denys Lasdun said that, by the time of *Galileo*, sound was very good in every seat. That may, technically, have been the case, but the reality was that John Dexter made as much fuss about the actors being heard as he did about any other single aspect of the production.

Almost as a point of pride, the National denied the use of amplification; but Green admitted they did try to 'boost' or 'enhance' the acoustics, particularly in what he called the 'difficult' areas of the auditorium. The problem here, though, was that sound was no easier to control than light; directional speakers were being asked tasks equivalent to producing beams of light so many feet long, which would stop dead exactly after that number of feet. And as Green and Lasdun both reasonably pointed out, sound is a subjective business bound to involve trial and error. Again, Green and the rest of his seven-strong team worked to very high standards. They saw it as their responsibility to adjust sound levels during performance, not just according to the director's prior instructions, but paying heed to any variation in volume at which the lines were delivered and such factors as the number of people in the audience and the amount of sound-absorbing clothing they were wearing. An audience of nudists, that is to say, would require a different sound level from a house full of fur-coated dowagers.

Green especially appreciated Hall's concern for sound quality and said they had a 'quite phenomenal amount of equipment'. The trouble was, his team needed silence in which to work. They could not ask quantities of people to wait around for them, so they had to squeeze their 'sound balancing' in during lunch breaks and late at night. Cue lights and similar equipment were supplied by them, as well as a TV monitor to help an actor with a difficult entrance in *Sisterly Feelings*.

Peter Radmore felt that his crew – who concentrated on lighting – also had less time on stage than they needed. Their job was to organise the 500 lamps in the Olivier so that, on every production, the lighting at later performances was exactly as the lighting designer had arranged it for the first night. Given the limited time available for change-overs, their rule of thumb was that two-thirds of the lamps remained in the same place, leaving one-third flexible for each show. On *Galileo* there was the complication of the rig they all so disliked, and the tension between the team – some of whom had been lighting designers in smaller set-ups – and Andy Phillips.

On Monday 7 July, Phillips had delivered a provisional plan of the rig, and they had started hacking up bits of aluminium barrel to construct it and had begun to cable it up. The next stage of preparation was the 'colour call', when the designer supplied a plan showing the code number for a particular gelatine colour against each lamp. Radmore then ordered the gels required. Even an overall effect of white light might need colour in some lamps. A very pale blue 'correction', Radmore explained, can be used to take the yellow out of incandescent light. As part of the first change-over after a production opened, his team would lay horizontal and vertical strips of canvas over the stage, thus creating a numbered grid they could use to record the position of each lamp. And theirs was one of the few departments at the National that actually did have a computer. They would feed into it details of each 'cue' (change of lighting) and 'state' to and from which the lighting changed. In performance, when the word came from Elizabeth Markham, the operator merely had to trigger the computer into the already-memorised cue.

The nine full-time and one part-time members of Johnny Pursey's props team possessed nothing as sophisticated. They did, however, run a small kitchen backstage in case meals were required as part of a performance. Everything that happened to a prop after it arrived in the Olivier was done either by an actor during the play or by Pursey's crew. But the latter were quite separate from the workshop department who actually made the props. Pursey's team stored, cleaned, maintained and mended props, as well as getting them on and off stage, being careful to avoid colliding with the stage technicians in the process. Demarcation was remarkably fine, but the different departments seemed to understand it. Candelabra that worked in the normal way, for example, were Pursey's responsibility; candelabra that worked electrically were Radmore's. These distinctions were not quite always observed. But in the change from scenes two to three of *Galileo*, stage technicians moved a rostrum, props people brought in chairs and a telescope, and electrician Charles Bata carried a lamp and placed it inches from that telescope.

They all wore white boiler suits, as did the dressers, and of course were indistinguishable to the spectators.

Pursey was a thoroughgoing theatreophile. One of his earliest jobs was operating the bubble machine for a revue called *Pink Champagne* at the Pigalle night club, and his brother was a backstage chief at Covent Garden. He tried to limit the number of his team on each production to eight, to make allowance for sickness and time off. While deputy master carpenter Roy Bernard had double this number available initially in the fit-up, his crew were divided into two groups only one of which was supposed to work on any given performance. After the opening, members of the second gang were filtered in as quickly as possible so that both teams would get to know the show. Far from being over-staffed, Pursey and Bernard exercised a good deal of ingenuity over staff deployment, and were often hard put to avoid bringing in extra casual help.

By the weekend before the fit-up, the small band of musicians hired specially for the production had had only three or four rehearsals under Dominic Muldowney's direction. For Muldowney, who ran the National's music department with fellow composer Harrison Birtwistle and a staff of two, *Galileo* was a missionary enterprise. He had long felt that Kurt Weill's importance as a collaborator of Brecht's was exaggerated, and dearly wished to rehabilitate Hans Eisler's reputation. He also welcomed the chance to supply more than 'background fiddling about' for a show, adding: 'Eisler's score functions as scene-change music, but it is functional, not cosmetic or incidental. The Eisler–Brecht relationship is a model of how a theatre director should use a composer.'

In a New Year meeting he had experienced little difficulty persuading Dexter to his point of view. 'Eisler influenced Brecht in a much more positive way than Weill. He set over two hundred of the poems, and kept digging Brecht in the ribs saying "This is not Marxist enough." His importance was political, not just musical.'

The choristers for whom Eisler composed presented a big problem. Muldowney felt they needed boys from an existing choir, as much as anything because a group from the same place would only need one chaperone and this would help cut costs.

Kevin Leeman
at the piano and
Dominic
Muldowney
conducting in
rehearsal

But where would he find them? During the spring, he had been giving a lecture at Roehampton and mentioned his dilemma casually to a teacher, who tipped him off about St Elizabeth's. Their choir master was paid by the National to rehearse the boys at the church, and he then placed them under Muldowney's rigorous baton in the production week. The music was three-part, so six was felt to be the minimum number for the choir. The master conscientiously selected a deputy for each boy. He was a little nervous of the play's content, thought Muldowney, being a 'straight Catholic', but there were no repercussions.

As for the balladeer, they had not known whether to go for a singer who could act or an actor who could sing. Opera singers as well as actors like Robert Oates were auditioned. The music – by a pupil of Schoenberg – was sophisticated, including much parody, but was for an unsophisticated character. Eisler was partly composing – in Muldowney's words – 'a musical definition of what a cabaret singer does all the time,' and there was the additional element of Brecht's beloved *Sprechgesang*. After recruiting Peter Land, Muldowney worked with him for an hour every lunch time during the first three weeks of rehearsal, then turned him over to Dexter. Along lines they had discussed, the director proceeded to 'muddy' the song by interpolations from the crowd. The object was to give the song a 'rough' atmosphere while minimising the need for Land to blur it musically.

The young composer recalled:

'We got them to do a Schubert *lied* at the auditions. We thought this would force the opera singers to cool the voice down and at the same time the actors could show how musical they were. We had these baritones filling the room with sound but I couldn't hear the words. Then Peter Land walked in. He had a strong voice, but in decibels, with less of the rich vibrato. And he had a solid musical feeling, intellectually as well as emotionally. As soon as he started, John and I looked at each other and I said "Let's stop auditioning, we're not going to get any better than that."'

Which meant that Peter Land could wave goodbye to *My Fair Lady*.

Dominic Muldowney conducts the choir (wearing plain clothes) in
their box in the auditorium

Rehearsing the ballad (*left to right*) Sandra Fehr (as the balladeer's
wife), Michelle Middleton, and Peter Land (the balladeer); with
members of the carnival crowd in the background

For all the excitement generated by rehearsals and now beginning to focus in the Olivier, there were as yet few at the National who expected – in their heart of hearts – that *Galileo* would be more than a *succès d'estime*. Brecht's dour image seemed difficult to reverse, and nobody was more aware of this than the theatre's publicists. 'I view any production like this as a source of concern,' said Alan Ayres frankly. 'The combination of Brenton and Brecht could put people off.'

Ayres was one of four young publicists inhabiting small, functional offices on the fifth floor. Each took responsibility for pushing a number of individual productions, selected on a basis of personal preference and informal bartering rather than exact quota. Their work concentrated on press relations and photography, and was only one part of the National's promotional effort. Within the same department were a copy editor and two graphic designers who produced books as well as the regular programmes. These extravagant-seeming appointments were made when Hall brought in his old friend John Goodwin as Head of Publicity and Publications, partly to reduce the large amounts then being shelled out in freelance fees. Over six years, Goodwin transformed an annual loss of £12,000 on programmes into a profit of £20,000. When *Galileo* went into rehearsal he had ten publications in the pipeline, only seven of which were programmes. His team also published the National's monthly repertoire leaflet, 120,000 copies of which were printed. But these were distributed by a separate division, Marketing, who handled the discount, educational and similar schemes.

On Wednesday 14 May Ayres worked out with Dexter by transatlantic telephone the blurb on the play for the August repertoire brochure. When the director arrived in London, it was quickly settled that Zoë Dominic, out of a number of top flight photographers, should be asked to cover *Galileo*. She was one of the few photographers Dexter tolerated, and so it was logical – as well as highly desirable – that she be invited later to work on this book. Her brief, apart from the book, covered shots of rehearsals, mainly for the early edition of the programme, and of a dress rehearsal. Of the latter, Ayres would distribute about a hundred pictures to the press, and make a selection for the front of house display. The publicist was required to collaborate with the director on this in case there were particular scenes that it was felt undesirable to show in advance. Pictures for the biggest newspapers were to be taken – at a special photo-call – and later sold, by an invited group of eight or so tried and trusted freelancers, a lucky elite to whom the National admitted new members at the rate of about one a year.

In the case of a production like *Galileo*, lacking a fail-safe ingredient such as a big star in its line-up, the imponderable but crucial publicity factor was the number of press stories – over and above reviews – that could be generated. The principal form of media arts coverage was the interview, but Ayres's most obvious candidates were reluctant interviewees. Brenton had recently had a lot of coverage, and the National wanted to save further exposure of him until *The Romans in Britain* – at that time, they imagined this would be harder to publicise even than *Galileo*. There were other 'names' in the cast – Andrew Cruickshank and Simon Callow were examples quoted by the publicist – but these two admirable interviewees had each enjoyed so much coverage in their time that they were now proving hard to sell. Ayres had failed to interest the colour supplements and glossy magazines in anybody except Gambon, and Gambon would not give interviews. There was a chance that Michael Thomas might stir some interest – the *Evening News* seemed a likely bet to Ayres – but this would only happen if and when he had won good reviews.

Increasingly, it looked as if any advance publicity was going to centre on Dexter, and here Ayres faced a tough proposition. Ayres had wanted to handle *Galileo*, having promoted *As You Like It* and being an admirer of Dexter's work, but he had no illusions that the director would lean over backwards to co-operate. In a long career, Dexter had learned all about the media's snobberies and other iniquities – one unsuccessful and one relatively successful production of his in New York were lumped together under an English newspaper headline 'Dexter's Double Disaster' – but for the Press Office life was a constant matter of letting bygones be bygones.

As soon as *Galileo* was announced, the *International Herald Tribune*, *The Times*, the *Evening News*, the *Evening Standard* and the *Guardian* let Ayres know they were interested in interviewing Dexter. The director responded that he would give one interview only, to John Higgins of *The Times*. This disappointed Ayres, as Higgins had already interviewed Dexter more than once. The publicist thought Tom Sutcliffe of the *Guardian* would have 'done something more incisive, asking new questions'. Ayres succeeded, however, in persuading Dexter to give a second, more down-market interview, and Michael Owen's prestigious 'News of the Arts' spread in the *Evening Standard* was agreed upon. Ayres then found himself on an extraordinary merry-go-round of Fleet Street diplomacy. *The Times* would have been miffed – possibly to the point of dropping their interview – if Owen's piece appeared before Higgins's, so the *Standard* writer had to be kept waiting while Ayres fixed up a time for Higgins and Dexter to meet. No less than five separate appointments were mooted, but each was unacceptable to either interviewer or interviewee. At one stage, Dexter suggested a breakfast meeting. Higgins said he could not eat breakfast and take notes simultaneously. Dexter suggested he just have coffee, but the writer declined. In the end, Dexter agreed to see Tom Sutcliffe as an alternative to Higgins. By this time, however, because Dexter was to shoot off back to New York immediately after the opening, the chances of squeezing in a later meeting with Michael Owen were slight, and so that interview fell through.

A potentially explosive situation was meanwhile brewing elsewhere. The *Sunday Times* was keen to interview Gambon. The publicist spent a long lunch break making a further effort to get the actor to relent and meet the paper. Gambon said no again, and Ayres 'offered' Dexter to the *Sunday Times* as what he called 'a consolation prize'. A colleague of Ayres had in the interim sewn up an agreement for *The Times* to see Dexter. Fortunately for Ayres, the *Sunday Times* then rejected Dexter and a clash was averted. But the production was proving more of a nightmare than he had expected. Ayres said:

> 'Dexter has to be handled very carefully. He'd tear a lightweight interviewer to pieces. He appears to regard publicity as a nuisance, and affects to despise pressmen. But when he got back to New York after *As You Like It*, he asked us to send over a complete set of the reviews!'

A constant stream of reports on advance bookings was supplied to Ayres, and he also kept in touch with Cassandra Mayer, his colleague handling press tickets. Over the first and two other early performances, 131 pairs of 'comps' were distributed, mainly to reviewers. In the circumstances, this was not an over-generous allocation. The National was always stringent about freeloaders, and differed from many managements in liking their first-night audiences to be as 'ordinary' as possible. Nearly two-thirds of the tickets for the previews and first night had been sold within days of the booking opening. Could this mean that the Brenton–Brecht combination was going to do good box office business, even with so little advance publicity? Nobody was yet ready to believe that *Galileo* might be a smash hit.

At the outset of my involvement in *Galileo*, Dexter suggested – with the National's endorsement – that I write the programme notes. The idea was to give me a small but practical relationship with the working process. At first, I hesitated. It seemed strange to take the fee of £150 – not over-generous for 2,000 well researched words – from an organisation I was supposed to be writing about with some objectivity. But then I decided it was up to me whether I remained objective, and went ahead. There were a number of demands to meet, not the least of which was concision. Dexter was eager that the programme reflect his 'hidden autobiography' idea, without telegraphing it. At one point, he suggested the text be confined to Brecht – mentioning the concessions the dramatist was deemed to have made to autocracy – with the illustrations devoted to Galileo. As I did, Brenton favoured written material on Galileo, and felt there should be some information about the destructive potential of contemporary nuclear science. Since in the play the astronomer's progress is pursued by the threat – implicit or explicit – of the Roman Inquisition, it seemed obvious that the programme should also refer to that body and its methods.

My diplomatically assembled copy was duly submitted. It was well received (though the *Spectator* later called the programme 'inadequate'). The National put its publications together as carefully as everything else. As well as copy editor Lyn Haill, my notes were seen by Dexter, Brenton, Hall and John Goodwin, even though the latter was then officially on leave. Word came from Lyn Haill that Hall disliked a couple of quotations. In the first, Lord Mountbatten spoke of the finality of nuclear war; in the second, a former nuclear physicist described the compromised behaviour of his erstwhile colleagues. Having already agreed to drop one quotation on grounds of length, and given that the coverage of the nuclear issue was already minimal, I suggested as a compromise that one of the two remaining quotations should be retained. There was no response, and in time the programme appeared without any of the contentious material.

When I later asked Sir Peter Hall about this, he said he thought inclusion would have been 'crass', though if Dexter had been in favour he would have given way. He went on: 'You have to be very careful with programmes. You can be taken down and used in evidence by gentlemen who ought to be doing a better job.' I inferred from this and subsequent remarks that he feared the critics might take umbrage at implicitly political content in the programme, and that this could be used as a stick to beat the National by the enemies of public subsidy. Hall's judgment demanded to be taken seriously. He was, after all, seasoned in such matters, and as the producer of *The Romans in Britain* could hardly be accused of wholesale timidity. But it struck me as a worrying comment on the theatre press, and others who make it their business to monitor theatrical activity, that they could not be trusted to deal level-headedly with one of the more enlightened pronouncements of Lord Mountbatten.

Chapter Thirteen

Week 0

Week 0, Sunday

The production week began at 9 a.m. prompt, with lumps of
the *Sisterly Feelings* set, giant black drapes, and short bars
('cradles') of lamps being whisked away into storage from the
back of the stage. When – as now – the real metal shutters were
revealed, so the good sense of using them in preference to more
artificial 'masking' became clear. This transformation scene
ceased almost at once, however, when something fell from the
flies with an ominous thud. The stage technicians marched off
immediately for a meeting, while Rodger Hulley, Roy Bernard
and others – looking distinctly sheepish – went into a huddle
at the point of impact. What had fallen sounded metallic, but
turned out to have been a plywood number plate from a lighting
cradle. The staff returned, but later work stopped again when
someone was spotted up in the flies and requested, in colourful
terms, to get out of the way.

In the midst of all this, Peter Radmore's team had pressed on,
unplugging the circuits that had fed the cradles for *Sisterly
Feelings* and connecting them into cables that were to supply
Andy Phillips's rig. This large but fragile rectangle was then
dropped vertically from the flies, and hooked horizontally beneath pulley blocks that had descended like monster spiders.
Since the rig came out beyond the fly tower and needed a lot of
support, the question of how its front end would be held had
been vexing Radmore. At the last minute, he had opted to
support it with winches behind some elegant baffles just over
the front stalls. Men from Kemp's had worked through the
night to install the winches – at a cost, Mark Taylor estimated,
of anything up to £1,000 – but the holes in the baffles through

which the supporting cables would be fed had not all been drilled. By now, Kemp's crew had gone to breakfast. Nevertheless, the electricians proceeded to fix lamps to the rig, threading them with the manual dexterity of a party of tailors. Soon the left-hand pair of the four front cables were attached and tensed, so that the weight of the lamps caused the downstage right-hand corner of the rig to bend alarmingly. Less than three hours after this morning session had begun, all of the lamps were connected and individual testing commenced. Only one did not work at once. When all four front cables were in place, the rig could be taken up to the height it would occupy for the show. Each of the winches had to be manually operated while the rest of the support was provided by the power flying system. Radmore carefully directed the operation with the aid of a loud-hailer. His men wound their winches frantically, but still the rig bent in different corners and the whole thing juddered violently before reaching its appointed level.

The stage was swept, and with a sudden surge of clatter and excitement the components of the truck and disc substructure were brought to the centre. Men congregated over floor plans, then swarmed out laying the track at the rear or linking weird parallelograms of steel beyond the edge of the stage. Someone started welding in the wings, and Kemp's team began hacksawing at the track to make a narrow gap where the shutter would descend. The truck was in three sections. After lunch, a dozen men lifted the first on to the track, and pushed at it gingerly. It moved a few inches without effort and as silent as a cloud. Meanwhile, the substructure had spawned all over the stage. The remaining sections of the truck were hoisted on to the rails and joined up in preparation for an important test. The truck was then edged along the length of the track, sliding easily over the substructure. A hint of self-congratulation seeped into the atmosphere. So long as the truck did not jam on the disc floor when it was in place, it looked as if its design would be vindicated.

Meanwhile, the 'Rome door', now flown three inches downstage of its position on Tuesday, hovered obtrusively over the industrious throng.

So far, only the central section of the aluminium structure surrounding the screen had been assembled. Now two more

Week 0, Sunday: a view of the
Olivier stage from the flies

With some of the *Sisterly Feelings*
mound still in place, the vertical
rig is lowered slowly from the flies

Now the mound is completely out of the way, the rig can be brought right down on to the stage
and made horizontal

The rig is hooked beneath the pulley blocks

The lamps are attached to the rig

As the rig is winched
up, it bends on the
right

The rig at its appointed
level above the stage

A portion of
substructure
positioned where the
disc is to reach beyond
the existing stage.
(This layer of the
substructure was to
give great trouble later
in the week and be
replaced by props)

The front and middle
portions of the track are
laid

The full length
of the track

Most of the
substructure is
now in place,
and the sections
of the truck have
been hoisted on
to the rails

The truck
is edged
successfully
over the
substructure

dangerously unwieldy lengths of silvery laddering were carried in. One of them was flown vertically and left twisting restlessly in the air. Throughout the day, the packed flies had been regurgitating objects: the screen itself came down and went up again, three projectors positioned for the galaxy effect at the end of the play took a couple of knocks as they too descended. And soon the poor old 'Rome door' had to come down again and return to the store. Mark Taylor declared that a third position was going to have to be found for the portal – as he had predicted against Hulley's judgment. It was still catching against the gauze screen from *Amadeus*, which would have to be 'brailed'. This crude but tricky operation required a line to be strung the width of the stage to pull the gauze back a fraction.

After the departure of the portal, its counterweight bar could not be removed. It kept catching against the galaxy projectors but these could not be shifted without adjustment to their electric cabling. Electric cabling could only be adjusted by electricians, and they had all gone home. In order to get the bar down, one of the stage technicians had to climb a 'Tallescope' and guide it with that highly sophisticated piece of stage equipment – a mop.

Lennie Thomas beavered away at the false shutter, and this was in time erected and tested. Even without proper lighting it matched the *bona fide* shutters extraordinarily well.

During the tea break, Taylor claimed that he and Roy Bernard would have to re-label the substructure for the crew's benefit. He still had grave doubts about it, and the first change-over from another show back into *Galileo* would be a tough test.

Cables were soon being flown up and down, some were hauled to the floor, and – in a moment of pure surrealism – a gigantic pair of wirecutters was lowered from the flies. At the same time, men were up in 'Tallescopes' and 'bosun's chairs' pulling into place the cross-pieces for the sides of the aluminium structure. The accident to John Mogford that had been avoided on Friday looked for a moment as if it might occur today, when one of the cross-pieces caught in the ropes of his chair. But he was rescued, work on the structure was completed, and the screen was finally installed. At 5.15 it was flown up for the last time, and very few people were left labouring on the stage.

Nobody pretended that everything hoped for had been achieved that day, but the sea of metal covering the stage testified to real progress. Roy Bernard stared at it thoughtfully. He turned to Mark Taylor and asked if this wasn't when Eric Dunn was supposed to be welding on the front feet of the substructure. And if it was, why had Dunn been allowed to go home? Taylor said he shared his colleague's puzzlement.

Week 0, Monday

Had lost time been caught up on during this second day, tempers might have flared less often; as it was, things fell further behind, and animosities hardened.

Before coffee, an uncharacteristically flustered Ric Green stormed on to the stage and took Rodger Hulley to task. His complaint was that a wire supporting the lighting rig was interfering with one of his 'reinforcement' microphones – or rather, with its protective cage. (Two of these mikes, worth about £1,000 each, had gone missing in the past – hence the protection.) Hulley eventually acquiesced under Green's onslaught, and electrician Andy Torble was despatched up a 'Tallescope' to remove the offending cable.

Then amid increasingly sour jokes about this being 'the last time', another attempt was made to install the 'Rome door'. Jocelyn Herbert had earlier agreed to a new position, further downstage than originally envisaged, but the portal could not be carried immediately beneath it because of the truck rails. Hoists were therefore lowered from the flies to lift the portal between the tracks, and it was trolleyed into place.

The counterweight bar on which it had earlier been hung was part of the manual flying arrangement; now it was attached to a pair of power-flown hoists. These took it off the ground smoothly enough, but it appeared to collide with the aluminium structure. Rapidly the portal listed to the left and it looked as if it might crash to the floor. Certainly, it was out of control. Those beneath skipped out of the way, but the portal remained aloft, swinging close to the screen. It was brought down again, noticeably wobbling. Back up it went after a small adjustment, but again it listed drunkenly. A fault had developed in the flying system and the portal would have to be manually flown after all. A warning was given out that nobody should cross the stage, and the portal was left trembling in its ungainly position while everyone went off for lunch.

Undaunted, or ignorant of the danger, Peter Land and Sandra Fehr – who played the balladeer's wife – took advantage of the break to rehearse on stage. The choir and band were in their box, while Dominic Muldowney commuted between there and the stalls, conducting the while. A cruelly comic possibility presented itself – that just as Land hit one of Eisler's higher notes, the portal might at last snap its cables and collapse on top of him. There was no such mishap. But the singers suffered because they were having difficulty hearing the band. The music was amplified, but only in the area from which it was naturally emanating. Across the expanse of the stage, this gave Land and Fehr an inadequate accompaniment. During a fraught rehearsal, they asked for speakers at both sides of the stage, for all this would contravene the policy of minimal sound reinforcement. Amplification eventually came to their rescue, but only after a few more anxious days.

After lunch, the 'Rome door' was lowered and carried off like a recidivist being removed to the cells once again. To release a counterweight bar in the latest-agreed position, the lighting rig was going to have to come down. With Radmore's deputy on loud-hailer, and four colleagues back at the winches behind the baffles, the desperate and delicate ritual of lowering and raising the rig was played out. This was delay enough, but the most drawn-out and fractious business of the day involved the substructure.

Before 10 a.m. the disc floor had been laid over the substructure; not long after, the truck floor was in place. But when the truck was winched forward, and despite the fact that there was supposed to be a three-quarter-inch clearance between the base of the truck and the surface of the disc, it jammed. The worst had happened. The cause was a matter of dispute. Everyone agreed that the adjustable legs of the substructure had been installed in a random manner. Taylor said this was why the disc was uneven and too high, and blamed Malone. Malone complained about unclear lines of liaison at National Theatre fit-ups, and blamed Taylor. The surface of the drum revolve was uneven, he added, and at the very front – beyond the edge of the existing stage – the substructure rested on carpet, so some late

Ric Green makes his
objection

Week 0, Monday
morning: the disc floor
is laid

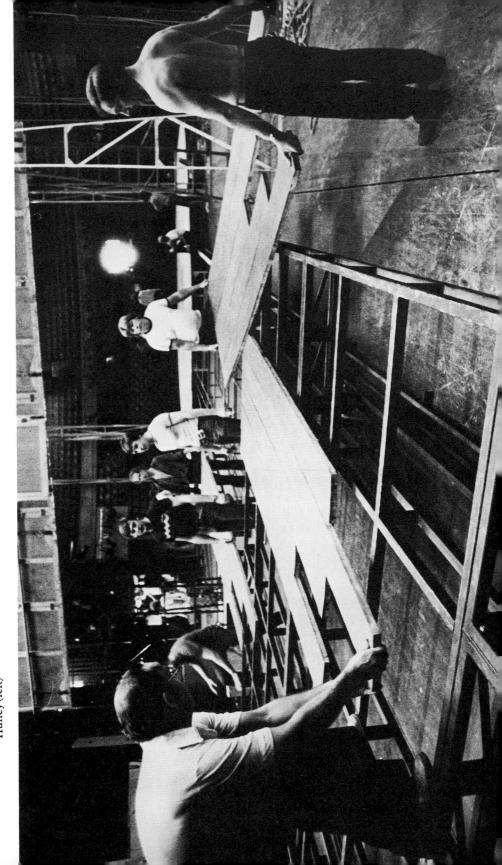

Meanwhile, at the back of the stage, floor boards are positioned on the truck under the supervision of Rodger Hulley (left)

adjustments were bound to be required. Malone further claimed, and Taylor denied, that the whole installation had been carried out three or four inches out of position under Taylor's command. Several inches had needed to be sawn off the disc because of this, so that important posts in the substructure would not be poised dangerously at an angle. Whoever was responsible, the floor boards would have to come up again and the legs be adjusted that afternoon. The crew was dispirited. One of them protested: 'Why didn't we do this fucking yesterday?'

'I know you've got big problems . . .' said someone to John Malone, as the day wore on. 'My problems are small,' he responded, 'they're Rodger and Mark.' His problems were certainly not over.

When the disc was in the rehearsal room, its supporting substructure had rested on the floor, which was even. In the Olivier, the substructure rested on the stage and beyond the front edge of it on the carpeted auditorium floor. The floor was lower than the stage, so an extra layer of substructure had been installed at the front to keep the disc there at the same height as that over the stage. The two front layers had been replaced later by wooden props. Now Eric Dunn was being brought in to weld metal legs in place of the props. The question everyone asked was why metal legs had not been used in the first place.

The electricians became embroiled in all this because they were due to start 'focusing' with Andy Phillips that evening. Climbing 'Tallescopes' to adjust lamps in the rig was not something they would look forward to if the disc floor was precariously supported.

Bill Bundy declared around teatime that they were two hours behind schedule. As for the workshops, he was worried that, having failed to use time effectively on Sunday, they had 'lost momentum'. Bundy was not the sort of general to conceal his feelings from the troops. Malone pooh-poohed his anxieties. The workshops, he objected, had been 'working their balls off'.

Galileo was treating Eric Dunn unkindly, though he remained chirpy. The substructure had mushroomed, taking 4,120 feet of steel, not the originally estimated 2,500 feet. The metal workshop staff had spent the best part of three weeks constructing its ninety-three components. Today Dunn had been called to weld the legs just when he was getting round to the armillery sphere. The missing hoop from the sphere – having finally arrived – had fallen over while Dunn was working on something else and cracked him on the head.

Week 0, Tuesday

Outside, the summer morning was fresh and warm. In the Olivier, with few people around and scant illumination as Andy Phillips tried out individual lamps, it was more like the aftermath of an evening show than early in the day. There was much sitting about in the stalls, and work happened in irregular bursts. But two major events occurred in mid-morning. The 'Rome door' was positioned at last and, after one false start, the truck was persuaded to glide smoothly over the disc floor.

It was a man transformed who continued the focusing of lights begun the previous night. The familiar cigarette still clung to his bottom lip, but now Phillips bounced around the stage, pausing on the balls of his feet in strategic places as if about to perform a high jump. As photographers consider possible shots, he would examine sections of the set through fingers shaped into a square: the idea was to ensure that where light from two sources joined there was no dip in intensity. He would also scrutinise the floor as if looking for specks of dust in a carpet: this was a search for 'discolouration', or marks on the lenses of lamps, invisible to the untutored eye. At the lighting console in the auditorium was a TV monitor screen that showed at a glance a plan, in the form of figures, of the lighting state then operative, and in flashing code reminded him of jobs to be returned to. Later Phillips arranged for a single, bare lamp to be flown down in the middle of the rig, giving an effect akin to the 'working light' in which stage staff habitually labour. This was his recommendation for the scene changes; next day, Dexter was to reject it soon after seeing it.

There was the smallest chink in Phillips's display of unfaltering proficiency when he turned and asked me if the box on the right of the stage would be used. Since this was where Robert Oates was to sit for his announcements, the enquiry surprised me a little!

At the back of the stalls, the bright young men of Radmore's team were much less impressed by Phillips, although they would move swiftly to co-operate when a job came up. They admitted that this rig – with less lights, and a diamond shape described within the rectangle – was more pleasing than that for *As You Like It*, but they clearly yearned for the chance to prove their superiority in lighting design. 'At the National you sit around waiting for someone to die,' said one, peering ominously in the direction of the busy little figure on stage. 'We're like labourers here. Trained monkeys.'

Their considerable ingenuity was demonstrated when the troublesome candelabra came on for testing. The flames flickered with remarkable realism, although they were in fact electrical. The effect was achieved by threading the wire feeding the bulb at the top of each 'candle' around a small spring, which wobbled when someone walking nearby vibrated the candelabra. The trick had been pioneered at the National and Radmore's people often fixed up props for West End shows with variations on the 'National Theatre wobble'.

If things travelled at a desultory pace in the auditorium, pressure in the workshops was escalating frantically. The assistant to the theatre's head of design passed through and remarked that she expected another strike within three months, such was the build-up. Yet scenic pieces needed for *Galileo* were now arriving only in dribs and drabs. The greater part of the set was gloriously in place – architecture in metal and timber to rival anything created in concrete by Sir Denys Lasdun – but problems that should have been solved by now kept surfacing. For example, the metal chassis for the balustrade had arrived but with a mistake in the measurements. Kemp's had constructed a second, smaller truck to travel on the rails from behind the shutters carrying the carpentered balustrade. But the latter was so weighty that to lift it on to the chassis was going to devour time and labour, even without the complication that the chassis – which itself weighed 3 hundredweight – was the wrong size. Somebody started talking about abandoning the chassis and flying the balustrade. This was interpreted as an attempt to broach the question that had so far been avoided: was the balustrade too heavy to be used at all? After a terse discussion with John Malone, Bill Bundy went off in search of Jocelyn Herbert to ascertain how attached to it she was.

The ramps up to the disc from the rear of the stage and the steps – or 'treads' – from the side vomitories and centre aisle were causing aggravation out of all proportion to their size. Carpentry begun on Sunday was still in progress. The 'vom' treads had to be completely secure: they were built over an existing set of steps that gave on to the floor of the stalls, but themselves had to reach right up on to the disc. The measurements to which their supporting metalwork had been made were wrong, and one of the welds had broken. This presented the actors with a long, nerve-racking journey merely to make an entrance. Similarly, the ramps must not remain unstable or noisy as this would sabotage important moments. The saga of the substructure legs rumbled on, and even Eric Dunn was now complaining. He claimed to have suggested a fortnight earlier that the disc be supported by props such as he had been asked to install at the last minute. Meanwhile, the armillery sphere had fallen so far behind that Yves Rassou was painting it in the metal workshop while welding went on simultaneously. But life had its lighter side. In the Collegium Romanum scene, a ceremonial carpet was to be laid from the centre aisle steps to the portal at the opposite end of the disc. On Saturday, Dunn had been asked to find a motor capable of propelling the carpet back under the steps after use. In time he had traced a machine that fitted the bill. But when he started phoning round, people responded as if he were off his head. They were only convinced otherwise when he explained that he worked for the National Theatre!

By teatime, Bill Bundy was agitated and perspiring freely. The centre aisle steps might seem a small item, but without them, he complained, they were 'up shit creek without a paddle'. The vom steps might have to be remade. The ramps were 'another cock-up'. An extra floor board had had to be fixed either side of the truck and he had brought somebody in to do this; yet when a week ago he had raised the possibility of farming out more work, his colleagues had been hurt. People were 'into empire building'. How, he asked himself, did you get people to work together co-operatively? On top of his professional worries, he had gone home last night to find that part of a walnut tree had collapsed against his house, pulling down guttering and breaking two windows. His face was long at the

One of the problematical ramps seen from the left of the stage

In the metal workshop, the armillery sphere gets under way at last

The 'pre-set', showing the completed armillery sphere in its position for the start of the play. (Pictured at the technical rehearsal)

Week 0, Wednesday: another hitch. Some of the scene one characters on stage with John Dexter. *Left to right:* Elliott Cooper (Lodovico), Michael Gambon (Galileo), Dexter, Marc Brenner (Andrea) and Andrew Cruickshank (Priuli, the bursar)

1609 - PADUA - 1609

best of times, but now wore an expression of unmitigated woe. Although he had spoken to Malone about the centre steps only half-an-hour earlier, he decided to go and chase them up himself.

Bundy's strictures were over-harsh. When people quarrelled, they usually did so over the best way of achieving high standards. No one ever said, 'This will just have to do . . .' That evening provided an example of the perfectionist assumptions on which business was conducted when, under John Rothenberg's guidance, the scene changes were attempted by the stage technicians, Johnny Pursey's team, and electrician Charles Bata. In the few hours available, they ploughed through three-quarters of the changes. The result was that, when the actors arrived on stage next day, they scarcely noticed their furniture and props were now being shifted by a different crowd of people.

Asked how he was feeling earlier in the day, Michael Gambon replied with mock moroseness that he had ordered his rubberised underpants. He would be wearing bicycle clips on Friday, for the 'death sentence' hanging over his head.

Week 0, Wednesday

Dexter had flown back from the States and, beginning at 11 a.m., was due to conduct a 'technical' rehearsal – scrutinising the scene changes, fitting actors into them, and working through the play on stage in time for an evening dress rehearsal. The armillery sphere – in place at last – gave an almost space-age finishing touch to the set. The musicians were in their box with the choristers tuning up. Deputy choirboys hopped in and out of the purple seats. Other people drifted in and out, testifying to the diversity of lives that were drawn together by the production: costumed actors, some with modern spectacles perched incongruously on their noses; Marc Brenner's mother and grandfather; workshop personnel and a large contingent from the costume department, anxious to know what late changes might be demanded. Andy Phillips wore headphones, and kept up a continuous dialogue with the lighting box. Peter Hall dropped by on a couple of occasions. A quiet but expectant hubbub surrounded Dexter, who laced the proceedings with juicy gossip about the Opera House murder.

Remarkably soon after the scheduled start, Rothenberg gave the 'stand by'. Robert Oates announced the play, the armillery sphere flew out, the truck began to trundle forward, and Gambon jumped up to take his place on stage. As he did so, Dexter called a halt. The truck was too noisy, he told Rodger Hulley; it should come on later and slower. Oates was asked to speak louder. The process that had just been seen was put into reverse, like a film run backwards. Some time later, they were ready to try the opening again. This time, Dexter stopped it because he could see an unauthorised spill of light above the band, and he was still unhappy about the noise from the truck. Bundy, Hulley and John Phillips discussed this, while a small altercation proceeded between Harrison Birtwistle and Dominic Muldowney over the exact direction in which the choir should face. Dexter had his head down, and kept spotting light where it shouldn't be. The opening was tried again, then again. As the truck slid forward this time, an extraordinary sight could glimpsed beyond the shutters: two burly, shirtless men strenuously heaving the winch handle helping to effect an apparently effortless transformation. It was an image that Brecht might have relished.

Again Dexter stopped the play before it had a chance to start, this time to talk urgently with Andy Phillips and Rothenberg. More light-heartedly, he ticked off Muldowney because the choir were not rising from their seats in unison. He asked that tabards and capes which might crease should not be worn by actors sitting in the auditorium. Pointing to one such figure, he asked Rothenberg the actor's name. Told it was Adam Norton, he muttered 'Might have known.'

For this opening sequence, Dexter had to harmonise an extra-ordinary collection of elements: as well as Oates, the sphere and the truck, there were music and song, two changes of lighting, the descent of the screen, the projection of the first slide and the entrance of Gambon and Brenner. It was not just a matter of getting the order right – the 'logic', Dexter called it – but of carefully timing everything through Eisler's extended musical introduction. Usually, scene-change music is too short for all that has to happen; in this case, the music was longer than the job took, and actors and stage staff were asked to stroll without

looking sloppy. Changes between scenes were no less complicated, and Dexter was not only concerned with practicalities.
For example, the dramatic 'high' at the end of each scene would
be punctuated by Oates's calling out the number of the next
scene; then there would be music, and only after that the rest of
the announcement. For all Brenton called him 'a Royal Court
humanist', this – like his dogged assaults on the final scene –
was Dexter endeavouring to reflect the Brechtian ethic.

After the tenth attempt at the opening, Dexter seemed happy.
Then instead of running the scene, as many had expected, he
gave the actors several minutes to wander about the truck and
try exits and entrances. Nothing else was taken over quite so
often, but gruelling reiteration was the order of the day. A little
after noon, they were ready to rehearse the transition into the
Venetian senate setting for the second scene. This was when
the tabarded Norton and company were to bear a canopy on
poles, but confusion broke out and as the lights went up they
were still frenetically trying to unravel which post belonged to
whom. As a result, the canopy looked as if it had been caught in
a gale and might blow away at any moment. Addressing Rothenberg, Michael Fenner said: 'John, would it be possible to have
the front poles labelled so that we know who should hold
which . . . ?' 'No,' interrupted Dexter. 'Easier is not better.' As
well as having to sort out the wayward posts in the darkness of
the wings, the actors were now finding that some of the 'gold'
was rubbing off on their costumes.

Just before lunch, Dexter called up to Robert Oates 'You're
acting too much.' Shortly after the break, demanding more
volume, he told the same actor 'If you've had one too many, go
and have a soda water.' The work ground on. Increasingly, the
length of time taken to 'set back' after an interrupted change
annoyed Dexter, and by the end of the afternoon he was urging
Rothenberg to 'push' and 'come on'. He still wanted more
volume from Oates, but was now communicating only in
gestures. Although the final scene-change was never reached, a
huge amount had been got through. Nobody had enjoyed the
day very much, but a number remarked how they valued
Dexter's ring-mastery. It had been only the second day the
actors had rehearsed *Galileo* in the Olivier, and their first there
in costume. Many other jobs remained outstanding – the stage

Attempting to sort out the canopy and other problems. Among those on stage are two boiler-suited stage technicians

Dexter (back to camera) asks what's going on during a hold up in the change from scene two to scene three. (Johnny Pursey is centre, in the dark trousers)

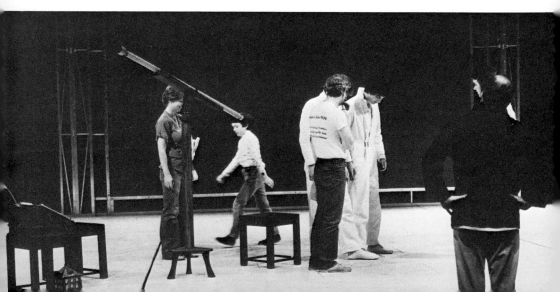

left area of the disc floor was dipping worryingly, for example. The upshot was that it was hard to believe a dress rehearsal would be starting at 7.30 that evening, let alone that the first public preview was on Friday. The National Theatre's production of *Galileo* had taken years to get on; now it all seemed to be happening too soon.

Rob Barnard – a member of Ric Green's team assigned to *Galileo* – professed himself content with the sound, crossing his fingers that Dexter would not notice the 'enhancement' of the choir. Johnny Pursey was happy enough, but frustrated in that the scenes themselves had not yet been played, so that his team still had to discover how long they had for repositioning between changes. Andy Phillips felt that he now had a 'structure' or style for the lighting, but only in a couple of scenes had the intensities of individual lamps been balanced. The scene changes, he now believed, needed a silhouette effect, but the necessary back lighting was difficult to achieve on the shutters: not enough lights were available to him, and light could not be thrown high enough. Dexter had commented that the armillery sphere needed to be lit more 'theatrically', so he had employed a criss-cross effect; something similar then suggested itself for the changes, although to Phillips this represented a compromise.

For his part, Dexter said that he did not expect the lighting to be right for a week yet, or even a week-and-a-half. He would be watching the dress rehearsal from different parts of the theatre, but for design and technical points rather than the acting. 'I've seen each of the performances peak already,' he added; 'I don't mind if I don't see performances again till Friday.'

Acting was important that evening nevertheless, if only to the actors. Gambon, for example, experimented with even more vitality in the earlier sequences. And when Andrew Cruickshank gave a more than usually ringing account of himself, Dexter said in a loud voice to Kenneth Mackintosh: 'Oh what the fuck is Andrew doing?'

For someone accustomed to the idea that dress rehearsals are carried out before a hushed auditorium, thereby recreating the ideal conditions of performance, there were several surprises. Dexter kept up a constant buzz of instructions and queries, passing comments to Mackintosh, and rounding up Phillips,

Tension in the stalls: Dexter (in the white trousers) and Andy
Phillips (right)

In performance: Robert Oates as The Speaker

Rothenberg and Herbert for animated discussions on what was to be seen on stage. Rob Barnard was summoned and told there was an unwanted echo. It came from the bare steel shutters, Barnard contended. 'Rubbish,' snorted the director, who suspected amplification. An unnecessary prompt was given, and Dexter leapt up to call in the direction of Neville Ware: 'That pause has been there for weeks.' When Andy Phillips told him that he had not yet worked on something, Dexter's voice rang out again: 'I'm not saying you have. I'm telling you what's required. If you'd care to give me a list of everything you've not done I'll be glad to receive it.' An atmosphere verging on panic pervaded the stalls while, by comparison, the great events being depicted on stage proceeded with a stately calm. With Mackintosh faithfully in attendance, Dexter watched the third scene slumped at the back of the circle with his feet on the seat in front.

A short, loud buzz came from the back projector just before the end of scene one and the screen went blank. This made for an odd comment on the new age of science that was being heralded below, but Gambon, who was speaking at the time, barely paused. At the beginning of the next scene, the appropriate slide came on, went off, then came on and – wobbling occasionally – remained for the rest of the scene. But it was impossible not to be impressed by the grip that was already being taken on the complexities of the *mise-en-scène*.

During the transition into the Collegium Romanum sequence, for example, ten actors had to find their positions on stage while a smaller group exited, Gambon's dresser came on to help him with a costume change, two of Pursey's team drifted down the centre aisle and unravelled the carpet across the disc, others brought on benches for the scholars, and stage technicians eased the descending portal into its exact position. All this had to be accomplished without collisions and while everyone kept clear of the retreating truck. If nerves were in the air, they scarcely showed. During his duologue with the Little Monk, Gambon asked for quiet in the wings; but, on stage at any rate, histrionics were confined to the acting.

In the interval, while Dexter and Phillips went into an urgent huddle in one of the front of house bars, Brenton commented that he hoped the production would liven up. Actors did not always seem to know why they were saying things or to believe what they were saying. At the Venetian senate, for example, nobody – including the actor concerned – appeared to know whether the Doge was 'a figurehead with the brain of a two-year-old put there by other people', or whether he was highly powerful in himself. Brecht contributed to the awkwardness, especially in the larger scenes, and the translator was reluctant to criticise Dexter's sometimes frustrated expectation that actors would 'bring things' to rehearsal. It might be old fashioned, but Brecht was old fashioned and his working method quite probably resembled Dexter's. And there were examples – Michael Beint as the treacherous Mucius, say, and Harry Lomax's ancient, fundamentalist Cardinal – where small-part actors gave the impression of having made some decisions about their characters' lives beyond what was given in the text. These were all too few, but perhaps over the course of the previews others of the lesser characters could be 'fired'. After some that he had worked with, Brenton admired and valued this director's discipline. The second run-through had been 'free but marvellously ordered' – since then, however, the production appeared only to have marked time. He would talk to Dexter.

Later passages of the dress rehearsal were more accident-prone. The Collegium carpet had left a great purple stain across the floor of the disc. In Galileo's study at Florence, the blackboard that had earlier bothered Dexter fell over twice without being knocked. The second occasion was at the climax of one of Gambon's speeches, and caused some titters among the cast. The bell rung to signal Galileo's recantation dissatisfied the director, and during the final scene he jumped on stage to change the position of Andrea's trunk and spread out the queue of emigrants. Back in the stalls, he told Kenneth Mackintosh 'I don't know what the fuck Michael Thomas is doing. He's nowhere.' Just in case the actor had not heard this, which was doubtful, Dexter later told him to pull his finger out. Thomas agreed he had fallen back a bit. The quickness of the scene change had disorientated him, and he was still getting used to the Olivier. Earlier, referring to one of London's attic 'fringe' theatres, Thomas had been heard to wail: 'I want to go back to the Bush!'

Surrounded by unashamed spectators, Andy Phillips and

Peter Radmore ended the rehearsal locked in confrontation. Phillips had decided he must demand additional lamps. He needed to focus more brightly on the perimeter of the disc, leaving a limited number of lamps for the centre; the middle of the disc required different lighting from the middle of the truck, although there were only a few inches in height between them, and so lights could not be doubled up. He had asked to use eight lamps, finely tuned, from the front of house area; the alternative, he said, was twenty more on the rig. Radmore felt he was being blackmailed. A score of lamps on the rig would mean a huge amount of work and he had doubts about getting power to them; but to employ eight more from the front of house would break his limit of one-third freshly focused for each show. Phillips should have worked things out better in advance, he maintained, and somebody might have thanked his team for all they had produced at short notice and by working through meal breaks. The lighting designer felt he was being treated to traditional blarney. 'We're not doing this for fun,' he told Radmore. 'Yes but it takes time,' replied the electrics chief with untypical heat, 'and it makes for a very long change-over.' This was too much for Dexter, who chimed in: 'Never mind, let's pretend we're doing *Amadeus* and do our best shall we?' Grim and tired, the director departed.

Next day, Radmore said he resented having been handed a 'shit session' by Phillips; it had been unfair to raise the matter when Dexter was around, because he was the kind of director who would immediately complain at the top level. Another director would have accepted more readily that what could be done was limited by the demands of other productions in the repertoire. One of Radmore's crew added that his respect for Phillips and co. had not been increased by their appearing to fall out among themselves. Nor, for that matter, by the fact that Phillips had managed without the extra lights after all.

Week o, Thursday

It was, then, a disaffected team of electricians who collaborated with Andy Phillips on stage for the first two hours of this morning. Dexter arrived at 11.30 to tackle the scene changes without actors. He looked no happier than twelve hours earlier and his voice at times quivered with strain. In tones several degrees above the conversational, he told of a phone call from Howard Brenton. 'Howard tells me he's not happy with the playing of some of the small parts. I've told him to take it up with the management and casting, there's not much more I can do in that department.' He then quoted a joke from the script. Looking through Galileo's telescope, the Doge spies some people eating and observes: 'Grilled fish. My mouth's watering!' How, asked Dexter, did Brenton expect the character to have more 'weight' with lines like that?

The first scene alone occupied an hour, without a murmur of complaint from the stage staff. The false shutter wobbled a lot, and the back projectors were again on the blink. In these mammoth machines, the weak link was proving to be the capacitor, a component of the starter units that moderated the inflow of current. The present wax capacitors were displaying an unfortunate tendency to melt. Rank Strand Electric had sent off to Austria for some paper ones that would, it was hoped, prove more reliable. After they arrived, however, each would take two days to install. This was typical of the binds in which Dexter's people on the one hand, and National staff on the other, kept finding themselves. The electricians considered they were working hard to provide back projection in difficult circumstances with relatively new equipment. But Dexter simply could not fathom why one of the most modern theatres in the world was unable to keep its projectors in operation.

There were more complex contradictions, too. Radmore and his team resisted some of Phillips's ideas because they wanted to keep change-overs speedy. Dexter objected to this, but at other times complained about the commitment of actors in the 'bottom half' of the company. Yet easier change-overs were crucial to the management's plan to improve incentive by staging more plays. As a further irony a number of actors – including Gambon – complained that the National did too many plays already!

Proper performances were not required of the artistes in the afternoon, when Dexter hauled through the play cutting from 'cue to cue'. Johnny Pursey was unravelling the carpet for the Collegium scene when he found he was about to get caught under the portal. Nipping back quickly out of the way, he tripped and fell on to the receding truck. This carried the giggling props man inexorably toward the bowels of the stage but he managed to jump clear before the shutter descended. Things were less larky for Robert Oates. His was a no-nonsense outlook, and he had for some time been promising to give as good as he got if Dexter kept up the aggravation. Now when the director called out yet another peremptory comment, Oates told him not to shout. Dexter summoned the actor down from his box to the stalls and explained that he had only shouted because he thought Oates could not hear. Oates replied, 'It's the manner I object to,' and returned to his perch.

As the treads were subjected to more frantic hammering, official photographers Zoë Dominic and Donald Cooper arrived to join the regular onlookers for that evening's dress rehearsal. Dexter had by now refused to admit the usual band of free-lancers, and neither would he agree to a photo-call. Nevertheless, the pair on hand kept up a constant clatter as they snapped away right through the play. Despite this, and the incessant murmur from Dexter in the circle and Rothenberg and Phillips on their intercoms in the stalls, the performances seemed to acquire a new *libresse*. Unbelievably, Gambon was finding more energy; Selina Cadell was colouring her characterisation more boldly all the time; and Elliott Cooper seemed brighter, too. Just when an inexperienced actor might have been expected to become overawed, or be tempted to conserve energy for the public preview on the following night, Marc Brenner went in the opposite direction. His understanding of his character's place in each scene was more intuitive than that of some of the more seasoned actors, and he kept finding new things to do. While the Florentine court philosopher was waffling on, for example, Brenner as the young Andrea caught the eye of Galileo's disciple Federzoni conspiratorially, yet without causing a distraction. Gordon Gardner was pleased with both Brenner and Timothy Norton, who would seek out the voice coach after each run and demand to be given notes!

Occasionally 'tutting' and shifting elaborately in his seat, Howard Brenton sat through the play again. Another scene that concerned him was the carnival, with Eisler's ballad sung by Peter Land. In its day, he said, the irreverence of the composition had given the song an outrageous impact. Now it was dated, and he was not sure if anything could be done about it. Brenton might have added that the crowd's colourful masks, dictated partly by the size of the company, contributed questionably to the 'realness' of the scene. To watch the actors rehearsing without masks was to see clearly that they were treating the rioters as slightly unhinged simpletons, so that while the scene was spectacular, exhilarating even, it was not exactly redolent of threat. In the radical magazine *Time Out*, critic Sandy Craig later specified a distance from 'present reality' as his single main complaint about Dexter's production. Had the people been seen less in fancy dress during this sequence, his objection might have been met. Perhaps the problem lay in Dexter's 'humanism', and the pursuit of an aesthetic effect based on Brueghel rather than something more subversive. Perhaps, as Brenton suggested, the music was just too anachronistic.

But the major event of that evening occurred during the first interval. While the choir rehearsed and electricians raced about with 'Tallescopes', Dexter bounded on to the stage and started pulling around various of the benches and candelabra that had been set for the ball scene to come. Nobody knew what was happening. Roy Bernard's crew had been trundling the balustrade forward with some awkwardness, but now Dexter waved it out of the way. After a few words with Herbert, he stepped off the stage bristling exultantly and declaimed 'Light that, Phillips!' Those in the stalls who had been gawping, in one or two cases quite apprehensively, now realised that Dexter had completely changed the setting for the ball. The balustrade was axed, as was the large candelabra with its 'National Theatre wobble'. What remained was skeletal and spare, but more in keeping with the overall design.

Later, Jocelyn Herbert explained that she and the director had discussed the change over tea. The balustrade had been mentioned in the text, and she had originally intended to reinforce its appearance with clouds and cherubs on a back projection. This had been dropped when they decided they were using too many slides, and the balustrade was left as a bit of an anomaly. The large gold candelabra had been meant to contrast with the slimmer, dowdier models in the preceding scene. But metal benches featured in both scenes, and indeed travelled 'anony-

Anachronism? Peter Land (centre, as the balladeer) whips up the carnival crowd

Week o, Thursday dress rehearsal: making changes to the ball setting, Dexter and Herbert on stage

The ball scene before . . .

. . . and after. In the foreground, Selina Cadell (left) and
Stephen Moore

mously' through the course of the play, so it was not illogical for the more ascetic candelabra to reappear in the ball sequence, too. At this stage, Herbert commented, you always pare things down.

At a stroke, two of the most troublesome scenic pieces had been dropped. Weeks of labour had gone into that candelabra, as well as much heartache. Roy Bernard thanked Dexter for relieving him of the hassle of shifting the balustrade, but everyone agreed that a production in the Cottesloe could have been mounted for what it alone had cost. John Malone later calculated that labour charges run up by Kemp's to finish the chassis in a hurry, added to the cost of materials, could bring the bill up to £3,500. Rodger Hulley said that he had persuaded Herbert to accept a two-dimensional balustrade at first, but she had changed her mind in favour of the three-dimensional model moulded in glass fibre. His version, he claimed, would have cost £40.

Dexter did not have many words for the company after the rehearsal. The frontier guard was proving an unlucky part, and he said to Glenn Williams – who had taken over from Michael Fenner – that his performance was 'too arms and legs'. Williams told the director he thought he wanted him to keep 'busy'. Dexter replied briefly 'Use your arms and legs but get it right.' And poor Artro Morris had caught his foot in the gap in the disc floor where the truck ran, resulting in a large swelling. Every time he lurched forward for the opening lines of the Collegium scene – trying hard to be 'weighty' – he landed on his painful injury.

Among the various conferring groups were the electricians. The slide had gone again in scene thirteen. To alleviate the strain on the capacitors, Andy Torble was soon going to have to work through the night to lay in a second main feed cable. The question was whether this would be enough to keep the projectors functioning throughout a performance, until the new capacitors could be installed. They were not at all sure.

Chapter Fourteen

In performance

Week o, Friday of the first preview

Until after the first performance – and sometimes not even then
– it is impossible for actors to believe that anyone will want to
see a new show. Artistes in the grip of post-dress rehearsal
nerves feel they cannot rely on advance bookings, the loyalty of
audiences, or the efficacy of publicity departments. It is as if
first performances begin before an empty house, and only if all
goes well may someone be out there to applaud at the end. It
was a bit of a shock, therefore, to discover that over a thousand
people wanted to see *Galileo* that night, and that some of them
had spent time standing in a queue for tickets. A sceptic could
see the turnout as exceptional nevertheless, because this was a
preview. Seats were cheaper and the critics had not had a chance
to interpose their judgments between actors and public. There
might be a few in this evening, but would anyone come, say, to
the second or third performance at regular prices?

As I collected my ticket, a fragile but imposing and vaguely
familiar old gentleman was leaning over the counter. He explained carefully to the clerk that he was with a party of four.
'Mr Dexter' had arranged for two tickets; he himself now
wished to collect and pay for the other pair. My hunch was
proved right by the name on the cheque the old man handed
over. He was Laurence Olivier. Having figured significantly in
Dexter's career and given the young Gambon work at the Vic as
a 'spear carrier', he had now come to see what they made of the
play – and the part – that he had turned down.

It had been a tense day, though the actors had kept their
peckers up. In a frantic race against time, Dexter had attempted
to rehearse each of the acts but in reverse order. Work on the

final scene soon bogged him down, however. Uncomplaining actors were pulled about all over to make the stage look crowded and to give the impression of emigrants receding innumerably behind the scenes. Eventually, Dexter told Mackintosh that more 'extras' would have to be brought in. Stephen Rooney had acquired a new 'mother' in the meantime and the director had shouted at Michael Thomas again. Gambon complained that he had never yet got through the Little Monk scene without noise from the voms. A sketchy curtain call was rushed through, the cast peeling away to leave Gambon on stage at the very end. 'One solo bow,' called out Dexter to his leading man; 'two when you've got some notices.'

An unusual hush descended on the theatre just before rehearsals broke at 5 o'clock, and suddenly less people were around. Dexter – dark circles under his eyes – sustained his vigorous duologue with Andy Phillips, however, and Gordon Gardner tenaciously patrolled the outer reaches of the auditorium taking notes on voice.

Around this time, floats for *The Passion* were scheduled to give an unannounced public dress rehearsal in the streets outside the National, and in the Cottesloe the fit-up for *Line 'Em* was getting under way. This meant that Rodger Hulley – who had been in the theatre since before rehearsals started – could not get hold of any carpenters. Most of the outstanding tasks on *Galileo* required carpentry. For example, to reduce noise that Dexter had complained about, more felt was needed under the treads and ramps. (A fire regulation required the felt to be covered with silk voile, but this was tardily observed during the labour shortage.) Hulley had already screwed the truck floor boards down further. The sound generated by the truck was the greater, he said, because Herbert had insisted on individual boards and these were beginning to warp in the heat. On top of that, the truck would take a hour to dismantle in the changeovers. Both problems could have been avoided if the designer had accepted the conventional plywood sheeting mocked up as boards.

Mark Taylor had been up and about early, too, draping gauze round the projection platform to prevent the bulb dazzling the back row of the stalls. A new Collegium carpet had been installed but this brought small comfort to the production managers. Weeks earlier they had recommended the same carpet to Herbert and she had turned it down. Rassou's team then worked on dyeing white felt closer to the colour she wanted but, as the stain on the disc floor signalled, they had not been able to persuade the fabric fully to absorb the dye even after hanging it up to dry for two weeks. The shade of carpet Hulley had favoured all along had been ordered yesterday and despatched from Huddersfield forthwith. But when they tried out Dunn's motor it shook the aisle treads so violently as to make it unusable.

The performers now dispersed into the warren of dressing rooms, never to come together again as a complete ensemble except when rehearsing or carrying out the curtain call. Odd individuals might only ever meet on stage in future, so easy was it to disappear in the corridors backstage. Gambon said he was 'frightened but excited'. Changing his tune from earlier in the day, he reckoned it was now about time the show went on. Dexter had told him to 'get on with it' and have fun, and he was looking forward to a brief sleep before the performance. Stephen Moore, by contrast, was restless. The 'Pope dressing' scene had lost, he felt, a quiet authority it had attained in rehearsal a fortnight earlier. Perhaps an audience would give him a stronger sense of how that scene was going. 'It will be nice to have a bit of attention,' he said. In recent days he had been 'just bellowing into an empty auditorium' in which there were a few odd people talking to each other: he impersonated Dexter asking, 'Jocelyn, do you think he should have another shade of red?' A lot of people did impersonations of Dexter – even Kenneth Mackintosh – but Stephen Moore's was one of the wickedest.

Marc Brenner was more respectful. About the director he felt 'better than ever now I know him better,' despite the repeated pressure from him over voice. Brenner's problem was tiredness rather than nerves, and he was counting the days to when he would be able to get to bed before midnight. His parents – whose lack of smugness matched their offspring's – had been struck by how self-contained he had been, and by his capacity to 'switch off' from the production at home. Dexter had taken them out for dinner and offered a little careers advice; they were 'over the moon' about how things had gone.

Of the approaching performance, Selina Cadell said: 'I don't think any of us know what to expect, and it's been made more difficult by Dexter being unnecessarily ratty.' Philosophically, she added: 'At this stage you lose all objectivity, all sense of what's good or bad. That you can't predict how it will go is no bad thing. You just have to swallow inhibition and pride, and deliver. It's like animals being let out of a cage into the wild.' Having committed herself to a full-blooded characterisation, she was glad that Dexter had encouraged her recently to bring some warmth to the penultimate scene, where Virginia is seen keeping her disgraced father under a stern regime. This had been a rewarding experience: without it she would have been angered by not getting so much as a 'thank you' from Dexter after dress rehearsals. Michael Thomas, too, had valued the director's most recent work on the same scene. It had given him something new to think about, and he would be less tempted to fall back in performance on what he had done before. Earlier this week his work had been 'straight out of drama school stuff' as a reaction to arriving in the Olivier, and Dexter had been quite right to jump on him. 'You've got to love that stage,' he realised, 'and believe in your right to be up there.' His routine for the next two hours was planned: 'Crap, kip, walk, warm-up, then that's it.'

Like Thomas, Elliott Cooper was looking ahead. He had decided it was a bad idea to try to reproduce the state he had been in on occasions when he had got his part right, even though at the time he might have told himself: 'Print that!' He had fetched up in a bunker recently, and with a lot of help from his fellow artistes he had got himself out. Now he simply resented having been susceptible to Dexter's 'vagaries'. A little apprehensively he said: 'This is the biggest thing I've done for years. I'm having to make up lost ground and take myself a lot more seriously.' He added with a smile: 'I've not had a drink today for the first time in ten years! But tonight will have to be an awful disaster to make me feel I'm on the wrong track.'

By remarkable contrast, Simon Callow – who was much more experienced than Cooper at sizeable roles in large auditoria – was not at all sure of himself. Continuing difficulties had dogged him, and he had failed to solve them.

'I've started to endow the character with an emotional background that's not in the script. I've decided he finds his father
impossible to deal with, loves his mother and has a terrific
crush on Andrea. Galileo is a father figure for him, just as he
needs the authority of the Church.'

This approach was beginning to bear fruit, but he was pursuing
it in a void. Some days earlier, he had twisted his ankle and
started limping. 'It felt terrific. I told John I'd like to use it in
the performance, but he laughed dismissively and made jokes
about Robert Newton and parrots.' Even Callow believed the
audience would help, however. 'They tell the story back to you.
They experience the story you have in a way forgotten, and let
you know how well you're telling it.' Perhaps grudgingly, he
acknowledged that the production's narrative clarity would
ensure some success.

From the first moments of that evening's performance, the
packed audience was attentive and appreciative.

Spectators at classy theatres tend to laugh a lot but often only
at the most obvious things. In this case, however, subtle turns
of argument – by the Florentine philosopher, for example, or
when Galileo demonstrates to Andrea how the earth goes round
the sun – delighted them. A kind of critical partisanship meant
that wry remarks by the decrepit Galileo raised laughs in the
otherwise sombre penultimate scene, and earlier a huge yell
went up when the Papal Astronomer said of the physicist's
discoveries: 'He's right!' The seams in Gambon's performance
were rapidly disappearing. There was, too, a strong shape to the
progress of his character's energy: in the beginning bursting
out of him; then burning confidently within; and finally, refusing to be extinguished. And Gambon persisted with his
search for the comic, cheekily shadowing the genuflections of
Cosimo's courtiers, for example.

Paradoxically in view of Simon Callow's disillusion, the
Little Monk's conversational scene with Galileo won a round of
applause.

A couple of incidents marred the company's joy. Near the
beginning of the third act, the slide began to wobble. Then,
during the recantation scene, Andy Torble – who, like Oates

In performance: the Florentine court visits Galileo's house. *Left to right:* Gambon, Michael Beint (Mathematician), Marc Brenner, Daniel Thorndike (Philosopher), James Hayes (Federzoni), Yvonne Bryceland (Mrs Sarti), Gordon Whiting (seated, as the Theologian), Jill Stanford (Younger Lady in Waiting), Timothy Norton (Prince Cosimo de Medici), Peggy Marshall (Lady in Waiting), and Edmond Bennett (Court Chamberlain)

and the choir, had remained exemplarily still in view of the audience – suddenly moved across his platform and ended up awkwardly straddling the projector. Just as Gambon made his most dramatic entrance, there was a fearsome buzz and the projector blew. The second foul-up involved Gambon, too. A misunderstanding led to his coming on too soon for the curtain call, and he had to negotiate his way round the frontier barrier. The actor later indulged in a brief shouting fit, the first time he had done so in the life of the production. Now playing the guard who operated the barrier, poor Michael Fenner got it in the neck again. 'I was furious,' said Gambon. 'You work all night and then get fucked about.'

In the Green Room afterwards, Dexter reported that Olivier had 'loved' the show and Hall was 'stunned'. He himself would say no more than that it was 'coming' but he beamed broadly. An equally pleased Howard Brenton proposed a toast to 'the dead man – Brecht'. The evening demonstrated, he believed, that the proof of the pudding was not in the eating. Some of the audience hated the play from the beginning, some loved it. In one of the intervals, he had heard someone say of Galileo's enemies: 'They were right. He was headstrong.' Brenton was not complaining: it showed the spectator had taken the point. This was perhaps not so true, on the other hand, of an American lady who had left the theatre saying: 'What an indictment of Italy! Wonderful!'

Week 0, Saturday of the second preview

One moment of acclamation at the first preview had embarrassed rather than gratified the company. At the end of the penultimate scene, loud applause broke out and a few people put their coats on as if to leave. The spectre of the border scene being dropped suddenly loomed again, and Brenton was one of the first to raise it. Dexter countered with some of the arguments he had found unconvincing at the supper at Jocelyn Herbert's.

'It is an optimistic play, but without the final scene it's sentimental and quasi-tragic. That tragedy was avoidable was

Galileo demonstrating to Andrea the movement of the earth round the sun. (The chair represents the earth, the boy a person on it)

one of his rules that Brecht never broke. The scene's
essential, even if there is a feeling of coda.'

He was surprised, he said, that Brenton was 'panicking'; perhaps he had been got at by his 'mates'. (Dexter seemed to
nurture an image of Brenton constantly emerging with fresh
mandates from conclaves of duffle-coated comrades.) The
debate was soon quashed with a simple but typically effective
stroke by Dexter. He kept the lights up at the end of the penultimate scene, and had Oates come in extra quickly with his
following announcement. The audience never made the same
mistake again. The frontier scene went better than ever that
evening, and even raised a few laughs. But Jocelyn Herbert
remained unconverted. As the public departed, she sat in the
auditorium saying: 'I hate that final scene. It makes me feel ill.'

The carnival incorporated a new idea Dexter had come up
with during the day. His problem was that on paper the scene
comprised little more than the words of the ballad, but it
featured the principal appearance of 'the people' in the play and
he wanted from it a powerful climax prior to the second interval. He asked the crowd to pursue the huge model of Galileo
up to the back of the stage and then pass under the false shutter
to dance on the bare truck. This innovation demanded fast work
of Pursey's team. They had to 'strike' the scene eight furniture
– representing Galileo's study – from the truck and then scurry
round to enter as supernumeraries in the climax of scene nine.
That evening they managed it.

The 'Pope dressing' sequence had also been subjected to
Dexter's drilling, though there were a couple of mistakes in the
performance and the audience spotted one of the robes going on
the wrong way. Nevertheless, the scene won a 'round'. Little
Stephen Rooney often arrived at the Pope's feet to discover that
one of the more senior 'monks' had dragged up a carpet, and he
became adept at kicking it back into place with appropriate
discretion. The screen and slide were not used in the penultimate scene, adding to its chill atmosphere. Gambon was
making more sense than ever of the final long speech. To play it
deadpan had been a courageous decision that was now paying
off handsomely. The argument that a life-enhancing revolution
had been scotched at the last minute was utterly credible. But

'He's right!'

the rest of his performance was not 'Brechtian' in the received sense of being austere. Rather, it was Brechtian in its relish. Gambon seized the part with both hands and, like Galileo at his geese, devoured it greedily.

For one person, however, *Galileo* was proving 'an unqualified disaster'. Alan Ayres had managed to secure very little publicity – as Gambon had forecast – but the publicist felt this was as much Gambon's fault as his own, and, even more so, Dexter's. A couple of hours before the second preview, Dexter told Ayres to cancel the Tom Sutcliffe interview for the *Guardian*. Ayres went back on Monday urging Dexter to reconsider but, he reported, 'Dexter cut me off stone dead.' The director relented, however, over photography to the extent that, during previews, he allowed freelancers to shoot from one of the boxes at the back of the stalls. But the only major press story on *Galileo* was an interview with Howard Brenton in *Time Out*, and the *Sunday Times* wrote to Sir Peter Hall complaining about the non-cooperation. Ayres said he understood Dexter might be 'terrified' of questions about the Met, but the director's attitude to public relations made him wonder for whose benefit Dexter intended his work. In an internal report after *Galileo* had opened, Ayres wrote: 'The impetus given to the production by the reviews should see it safely through September/October, but the winter could see it requiring a fairly heavy advertising push.' When Dexter worked at the National in future, he recommended a guarantee be extracted in advance that he would offer 'proper facilities'.

Now members of the props team were providing emigrants as well as rioters, Johnny Pursey decided to 'put in' for more money. After a conference between stage controller Andrew Killian and Michael Hallifax, this was agreed. Shifting scenery in their 'blacks' was seen as a regular part of the stage staff's job. When they were more integrated – as they were in the white boiler suits for *Galileo* or if they dressed up in wigs for Restoration comedy – they received an 'appearance fee' on top of their salary. Similarly, actors were paid extra for helping move scenery. When stage staff contributed more actively to the drama – as they did tossing a dummy Cardinal in a blanket in the carnival riot, or shuffling along in the queue on the frontier – they received an additional amount for 'artistic input'. But

In performance: the 'Pope dressing' scene. Basil Henson (as the Pope), Stephen Rooney (at the Pope's feet, holding out a mirror), and Stephen Moore (left, as the Cardinal Inquisitor)

here the ice was thin, because what they could not do was actually act – that was work for members of Equity. Hallifax and Killian gambled that they would not incur objections from the actors' union: the National provided a lot of work for its members, and the union knew the theatre was 'on the level'. Accordingly, the £3.23 per performance appearance fee was upped in view of 'artistic input' to the princely bonus of £4.88 per performance.

With fifteen minutes to go, all seats for the second preview had been sold and about a dozen people turned away. Somebody booed at the end – to be promptly slapped by his companion – but the reception was generally better than the night before, and the audience seemed to have followed it even more closely.

Monday of the third preview

At the conclusion of the exhausting carnival rehearsal on Saturday, the actors had flopped out all over the stage – some removing odd bits of clothing – to hear the director's notes. Suddenly Dexter interrupted himself to announce that they had just given him a picture with which to open the scene. This morning, he inserted the image of a crowd enervated after a day's revelling in hot sun, before the balladeer enters to revive them.

This sequence was now obsessing Dexter as much as the frontier scene. Additional flags and banners were hastily introduced. Dexter continued to do 'traffic' work, experimenting with timings for the arrival of different components in the carnival procession. When the arms of the great Galileo figure opened, he asked for the music to cut and the crowd to freeze, but this didn't work. He chopped and changed with various individuals, keeping some of them downstage of the model at the end. Adam Stafford appeared as a young pauper with a wooden leg. Dexter built up his part so that he was left centre-stage spinning round as best he could.

After these exertions, John Rothenberg unexpectedly handed out sheets to the cast. They found themselves being asked to sing the choir's song from the close of the play, a 'warning' to the audience about the uses to which science may be put. Something was missing from the ending, Dexter explained, and he suspected it had to do with the force and clarity with which the song came over. The new idea was to begin with the choir and bring the entire on-stage cast in for the very last stanza.

At a hastily called music rehearsal later, Muldowney coached whoever was available in a 'detached' vocal quality. Back on stage in the afternoon, he urged the full cast to keep the song at a 'friendly' level. Dexter added: 'Keep the bite, but sing softer – act a bit more danger.' Then he asked them to speak the lines in rhythm; then to speak adding a tone of warning; then to whisper. Next they sang it turning toward the audience – 'absolutely artificially' as Dexter put it. And again, giving full volume to the final line.

It looked perilously crude in the cold light of afternoon and without costume. Indeed, the direct turn to the spectators was later dropped. But Dexter thought for a moment, then said 'Yes, buy that,' and the singing was 'in'. Surprisingly, nobody much minded the extra labour, nor the lateness of its introduction. Rightly as it turned out, most of the cast thought it would help.

Occasional lines were still being changed by Brenton – Andrea now reported to Galileo in their final meeting that Descartes had 'thrown' rather than 'stuffed' his treatise on light in a drawer – and added to the border scene. Rodger Hulley remained preoccupied with the truck. Having waxed it at Herbert's request the week before, he now had to have the wax removed as the actors were finding the truck floor slippery. On his platform, Andy Torble was to wear black instead of the more fetching white boiler suit. This meant that if the projectors needed first aid again, he would be less of a distraction, and that – during the long scenes with which he was becoming increasingly familiar – he could read his magazine more discreetly, too.

At a slightly adjusted curtain call that evening, there were loud cheers for Gambon. Peter Land now appeared in the line-up of principals, and there was an acknowledgment for the choir and band. As yet, Robert Oates was not being featured, but this – everyone assumed – was an oversight Dexter would be correcting before Wednesday.

Tuesday of the final preview

The next day only held more aggravation for Oates. At lunch time he ran into Dexter outside the Green Room, and was shattered to be told that neither Dexter nor Hall liked his work as The Speaker! If he could replace Oates with captions, Dexter added, he would. The actor was then ordered to spend a couple of hours that afternoon working separately with Gardner.

The Speaker's announcements were intended to relay information in a crisp but neutral tone. As Gardner pointed out, it was not easy to combine this with the projection necessary in the Olivier. Television newsreaders might evince a kind of neutrality, but they didn't have to raise their voices. Gardner felt Oates was 'singing', and Brenton thought he sounded cross. Later, at the official first night, theatre archivist Raymond Mander said Oates resembled 'Lilian Baylis with a beard'. But the actor was by now so befuddled with comments and indecipherable silences on Dexter's part that he did not know what was required. He had been made some kind of scapegoat, he believed, and dreaded getting the sack.

While the private session was in progress, Kenneth Mackintosh read the announcements from the stalls at the main rehearsal. Since each scene-change was proceeding as in performance, the light was still being brought up on Oates's box. This was now empty save for the actor's unoccupied chair, and a rather chilling image presented itself that seemed to echo Oates's worst fears. Toward the end of the afternoon, Oates returned to the auditorium but could not bring himself to resume his place. Mackintosh continued to read in for him while the actor lurked at the back of the theatre looking thoroughly miserable.

For the rest, the atmosphere veered between a slightly reckless cheer and grim anxiety. Dexter was working through the play, again concentrating on the carnival and frontier sequences. One moment he was 'conducting' the band or playfully cuffing Andy Phillips, the next he was wrangling with Rothenberg over the timing of a cue: 'Get on with it, get on with it,' he snapped at his old friend. Dexter had told Brenner after the previous night that his performance as Giuseppe was 'a wreck'. Now he urged him not to 'act' too much, to play it more naturally. Brenner looked sheepish, but his father insisted the pressure was not upsetting him. The final song had been the subject of a heated debate between Dexter, Brenton and Muldowney. Clarity of message was the bugbear, and Muldowney insisted that this could be improved with existing resources. He had already started re-arranging some of the earlier verses giving the soloist more to do. This afternoon the closing song was rehearsed so that it began with the soloist, continued with the whole choir, and ended with the company. This was the arrangement they settled on in the end. The choir made up for any depletion in their role by rendering 'Happy Birthday' to one of their number over the theatre's tannoy at teatime.

After rehearsals, Roy Bernard observed that the disc was still bending excessively and the treads remained troublesome. He also nursed serious doubts as to whether they would ever be able to put the substructure together again. The auditorium was a frenzy of activity. The back of the stage was being washed, and Phillips continued the lights focusing that had been resumed in the morning. Radmore's men wheeled out the 'Tallescopes' and started yanking about the huge 'galaxy' projectors. Dexter had complained that the image was not panoramic enough, and Radmore resented Andy Phillips's apparent lack of concern about this problem. Herbert later agreed that there was con-fusion over whether she or Phillips was responsible for the galaxy. Mark Taylor had suggested that the projectors could point crossways instead of directly down on to the shutters, thus, being further away, producing a wider image. But Radmore reckoned the projection needed to be not larger but more spread, so they reduced the slide size, projected at a wider angle, and scratched in some more 'stars' at the ex-tremities of the slides. Dexter remained dissatisfied. While Taylor's idea was being tried out, he dropped into the audi-torium and summoned Bill Bundy for a whispered consulta-tion. A despairing Bundy reported that the director had threatened to cancel Wednesday's performance if there was no improvement. He then turned to me and said, 'I hope you enjoyed that.'

Just then, as had happened several times during the week, a crowd of sightseers was shepherded into the circle by one of the National's official guides. Somebody remarked wryly that the

party was no doubt being informed how wonderful and satisfying it was to work in theatre.

Marc Brenner's parents brought eighteen friends and relatives
to the final preview that evening, having applied too late for first
night tickets. They were a sober crowd – Brenner senior ordered
five tomato juices at the first interval – but they admired the
show. Howard Brenton, too, was happy, feeling that the Church
was coming over more strongly. He had been finding himself
strangely obsessed by the play and had been unable to work on
anything else recently. In the penultimate scene, when Andrea
discovers that Galileo's survival has enabled him to finish his
masterwork, the pupil's tone changes abruptly from condem-
nation to praise. 'Even in the field of ethics,' he tells Galileo,
'you were centuries ahead of us.' The audience clearly enjoyed
this and other ironies. But what about the odd catcall? This very
probably indicated – in Brenton's words – that people were
responding to the play in terms of what it dealt with rather than
as a piece of theatre. For the company, of course, it would be
nice to know they were associated with a hit. Time – more
specifically, tomorrow's official first performance – would
tell.

Wednesday of the official first night

Pre-opening stress did not inhibit the considerable generosity
of Dexter and others. The director had brought a gift from Paris
for little Michelle Middleton, and at lunchtime laid on a
champagne buffet in Rehearsal Room 2. Stage staff as well as
actors were invited to quaff bubbly and consume elegant sand-
wiches. Michelle herself made cards for everyone. Adam
Norton took a taxi to Hamley's in search of a kaleidoscope for
Gambon. On reaching the store, the young actor discovered that
kaleidoscopes were out of stock, so he settled for a map of
seventeenth-century Europe. Norton was not sure about his
own contribution but thought the show was going to be 'great'
and he 'couldn't wait to hear them clapping at the end.' At the
buffet, he received his first 'note' from Howard Brenton.
'Remember,' the author said, 'that you are the voice of the
Middle Ages.'

In performance: the frontier scene. Marc Brenner (extreme left, as Giuseppe), Michael Thomas (seated, as the older Andrea), Adam Stafford (centre, as one of the superstitious boys) and Glenn Williams (right, now playing the frontier guard)

Star in the making: Michael Gambon as Galileo in the penultimate scene (pictured before the slide was dropped)

Peter Radmore had decided it would be hypocritical to attend and stayed away.

Every corner of the National's five-acre site might not have been brimming with excitement about *Galileo*, but there was a general air of nervous good will. A special table was laid out at the stage door, where a free poster advertising the play and at least a dozen good luck cards awaited each of the actors. Many artistes sent first night cards to everyone else in the cast, and the whole ritual threatened to get out of hand. The problem was that if you decided to send cards only to your friends, at least one person you omitted was bound to be upset!

Sir Peter Hall sent cards too, invariably signed 'Peter'. In the old days, he had sometimes added his surname in brackets, but this only earned him the nickname 'Peter Brackets Hall'. Now he had wisely had cards printed with his full name at the top. Nothing extravagant, just compliments slips. And Hall, like everybody else who had contributed to the production, received two coloured duplicated tickets. These were redeemable at the Lyttelton bar after the performance and were an alternative to the management throwing a party. The blue ticket entitled you to a glass of champagne, the yellow to a glass of wine. As for teetotallers, there was rumoured to be a black market in the chits.

Gordon Whiting muttered that he didn't know why people came to first nights – they never saw a show at its best. He had enjoyed the last week-and-a-half less than earlier rehearsals, finding the constant repetition exhausting. Michael Thomas, by contrast, was very happy, despite a dressing down from Dexter when he tried to conserve his voice for the evening. Thomas received a copy of Christopher Isherwood's *My Guru and His Disciple* from, of all people, his agent. 'Agents can be surprising sometimes,' commented the actor. Marc Brenner was feeling fine, and not nearly as nervous as he had expected. Timothy Norton was highly nervous. Although he had been in plays at the National before, this was to be the first time he had spoken lines at a première. Elliott Cooper was excited, tired, and looking forward to it. Stephen Moore said he was not nervous, but thought he ought to be.

For Selina Cadell, the production was proving an experience such as she had not known before. Partly because of the separateness of each scene, she found it impossible to gauge how a performance was going. 'No sooner have you established something than it's gone,' she mused. No feedback came from the audience to help. Her isolation was exacerbated by the nature of her role. A lot of what other characters felt about Virginia remained unknown to her, so the actress again had nothing to work on. 'I almost feel by the end of the play people haven't noticed Virginia. I think in the curtain call – why am I standing here?' She was not complaining, though: she assumed it all had to do with Brechtian alienation. But neither could she claim to be enjoying herself. On stage she felt enormously self-conscious, and she was sick with fright before each performance. Gambon and she would huddle together before their third act entrance telling each other it was going well – but without much confidence.

The leading man himself managed to appear calm, though in reality he shared Cadell's experience of performance. His bowels had given cause for concern in recent days, he said, and he was contemplating replacing the rubber underpants with a diving suit. He suspected that the 'fourth floor' (which housed the upper echelons of production and management) were surprised how well *Galileo* was working, and that they didn't really like it themselves. The design department, in his assessment, were particularly awed by Jocelyn Herbert's achievement. 'They're cunning on the fourth floor, you have to watch them.'

Rehearsing that afternoon, Dexter continued to worry at things large and small. On the first, ominous entrance of the Cardinal Inquisitor, Stephen Moore appeared dressed in the usual hat, gloves and shoes, but in place of his ecclesiastical robes he wore his running shorts and vest from *Sisterly Feelings*. Nobody was quite sure what Dexter's reaction would be. The director walked silently down the centre aisle, and stepped on to the stage. He went up to the delinquent actor, pulled at his shorts, examined his backside, then called up to the lighting box 'Blackout!'

Appropriately, the afternoon ended with the frontier scene. There had been trouble keeping the barrier stable when Marc Brenner leant on it to examine the galaxy. Mistakenly, Dexter thought Michael Fenner was forgetting to tie down the post after it was last raised. Concluding the rehearsal, Dexter said:

'And Michael, try not to let the barrier fly up.' Fenner began to explain, but the director cut him off and called out to everyone, 'Right! See you next year.'

That was the last most of the actors saw of him.

Perhaps the most remarkable thing about the official first night was that Gambon managed to perform even better than before. Despite the tension of the occasion, he injected yet more sheer delight into the pioneering Galileo of the early scenes, and pointed up the later ironies more sharply still. Fresh things were happening all the time, particularly in his relationship with Selina Cadell. The actress effected a ripening of performance just when it most mattered, as did Basil Henson. One might have expected a couple of actors in such a large cast to be working below par, but no one was. Adam Norton, for example, brought an appreciable hush to the auditorium in the troublesome Collegium sequence. Even the young choir were biting on their words with as much energy as they devoted to the plates of canteen chips. Dexter had shortened the carnival music, and this enabled him to bring the elements of the procession in quicker succession and to more dazzling effect. Although there was now merely one slim candelabra in the ball scene, it achieved an odd sumptuousness.

The performance was not without mishaps. There was nearly a catastrophe when the 'Rome door' was lowered in advance of scene four instead of scene five. It looked as if the portal must collide with the advancing truck, but it stopped a few feet above it and then rose demurely to be replaced by the screen. But nothing could mar the triumph. Standing ovations are almost unheard of in the theatre these days, but several of the audience were brought to their feet at curtain call, with yet more cheers for Gambon.

They had done it. Dexter, Herbert, Brenton, Phillips, cutters and stage staff, electricians and actors – they had brought alive for an English audience the 'dead man's' masterpiece.

Many of the non-actors most closely involved had been too agitated to sit through the show. Dexter had prowled the front of house like a cat on hot bricks; Brenton, Herbert and Radmore retired to the bar during the third act for a heated discussion on the merits of the final scene. As the audience were leaving, Hall and Brenton grabbed the chance of a quick chat about a pressing

problem – who would play Caesar in *The Romans in Britain* –
but they were both clearly excited by the success of *Galileo*. Hall
remarked that he had never thought himself able to direct the
play as well as Dexter, and that the evening had confirmed his
judgment. As for the new star, Sir Ralph Richardson called him
'The Great Gambon' and this set Hall thinking of parts Richardson was famous for that Gambon might play. He instanced
Falstaff 'in five years' time – maybe less'. Certainly, he had witnessed another actor's turning-point. Later, Gambon said Hall
wanted him to play Henry V. With his usual self-effacement, the
actor suggested he was too tubby for the role.

Gambon turned up in the Lyttelton bar, pallid as ever,
obviously discomfited by the attentions being heaped on him,
but making an effort not to duck out. Dexter had called in his
dressing room ten minutes before the show and repeated: 'See
you next year.' Few people expected the director to appear in
the bar afterwards, and he did not.

As for the reception given to Gambon in the dressing rooms,
one of the nicest aspects of this was that at least eight different
individuals came up to me to make sure I knew about it. Whatever might be omitted from this book, they were determined
that Gambon's backstage ovation would be included.

But Robert Oates never did get his curtain call.

Chapter Fifteen

Afterwards

Three-and-a-half years earlier, following bitter experience, Gambon had resolved never to read reviews. 'If they're good they distort you,' he explained. 'If they're bad they make you cry. So why bother?' On the morning after *Galileo* opened, however, someone had 'pushed the *Daily Mail* review under his nose' and he had read himself described as entering 'that small, charmed First League of his profession'. He dismissed this as 'flattery' and was not tempted to read more.

By the time the Sunday and weekly reviews had been added to the dailies, there were as many unfavourable – to the play, at least – as positive. The distate for Brecht as myopic and crude was expressed in terms depressingly similar to those used to deprecate socialists outside the theatre. Critics who saw themselves as more sympathetic to Brecht nevertheless inclined to regard the play as a self-portrait. Some of their comments – John Elsom wrote in the *Listener* that 'Brecht, like Galileo, was a survivor' – echoed Dexter's ideas with appreciable precision. During the previews, Dexter had said: 'The approach to Galileo in the light of Brecht has paid off enormously in giving it subtextual depth.' But Brenton thought the director had forgotten all about such notions, and they were not, truth to tell, often mentioned by Gambon.

A number of other plaudits were especially rewarding in view of work that had gone before. In *The Times*, Irving Wardle praised the serious presentation of the Church, and, like a number of his colleagues, spotted Gambon's adroitness in the ageing process. About Dexter's production, Felix Barker wrote in the *Evening News*: 'Never before in my experience has a play by Brecht been presented with such definition or clarity.' There were remarks on Jocelyn Herbert's work that she might have penned herself. Bryan Robertson told *Spectator* readers of her 'superbly elegant props . . . and mostly restrained costumes, which perfectly reflect Brecht's desire for scenes . . . that offer a convincing sense of time and place but do not allow the audience to forget that it is in a theatre.' Just as Lasdun was later to say that they 'understood the nature of the space very well', so James Fenton wrote in the *Sunday Times* that Dexter, Herbert and Phillips 'show off the Olivier as a marvellous theatre, as opposed to a concrete white elephant'. The same critic found the production 'a great work of art'.

Jocelyn Herbert said that she would normally take it as a mark of failure for a set to be noticed and she still believed that if the disc had come further out it would have rested more perfectly in the bowl of the auditorium. But she conceded that her design might provide 'some good guidelines for the future,' and thought the Olivier had at last 'become one place'. However, she was alarmed to learn that, once again, a meeting had been called to discuss her plan for the new stage. Her suggestions were only ever meant tentatively, and *Galileo* held lessons – Dexter thought the disc was too high, for example – that must be absorbed before anything was built.

Praise for Gambon left little space in the 'major' reviews for the rest of the cast. Selina Cadell was the most frequently mentioned of the others. A few of the critics singled out Basil Henson, Simon Callow and Stephen Moore, though the two last-named had their detractors as well. Michael Thomas and Peter Land received one nice 'mention' each, but there was not a word for Marc Brenner, Elliott Cooper or anyone else.

Stephen Moore remained discontented and was not at all sure he would ever crack the 'Pope dressing' scene. He had raised some laughs, which the *Observer*'s Robert Cushman referred to with cruel irony as Ayckbournian. Moore commented: 'You've got to put on a bit of a show for the punters – can't let them know you're unhappy.'

The choir had been found 'unintelligible' by some, and this deeply upset Dominic Muldowney. He felt that the boys were very clear – 'they're enunciating to the point of being unmusical,' he muttered – but the audience were distracted by the scene-changes. Dexter was on his way back to New York to resume work on a new Jule Styne musical, so Muldowney raised the matter with Hall. The only solution they could come up with was to amplify the choristers even more.

The second official performance was given on Thursday 14 August. That morning, Mark Taylor took advantage of the post-opening lull to spring-clean one of the fourth floor offices. From noon onwards, members of the *Galileo* cast were caught up in a succession of rehearsals for understudies and replacements in *Amadeus* and *Othello* which continued right through to Saturday afternoon. Gambon found himself plunged into a sort of 'post-natal' depression and developed sinus trouble. But Johnny Pursey pronounced himself delighted with *Galileo*, which had brought actors and stage staff together in a manner he had not known before.

At the end of the week, John Goodwin asked to see Gambon and again tried to persuade him to talk to the *Sunday Times*. Gambon was disturbed by the idea that he might positively damage his career if he did not give an interview, and was moved by the importance of helping his employers. But after thinking about it, he held his ground. A little caustically, he pointed out to Goodwin that only three performances of *Galileo* were scheduled for October; they couldn't need much more publicity to fill three houses after the reviews they had picked up. 'He went a bit quiet when I said that,' reported Gambon.

By this time, the National was busily arranging for *Galileo* to remain in the repertoire beyond its originally planned close in February. The third and fourth performances were packed – fifty-one standing positions being sold on Wednesday 20 August – and Stephen Sondheim and Harold Prince were among the luminaries who, as is the habit of luminaries, flocked to see the latest success.

When *The Romans in Britain* opened, with many *Galileo* actors in the cast, Sir Horace Cutler of the Greater London Council and Mrs Mary Whitehouse of the mysterious National Viewers and Listeners Association loudly vilified it. As a result, the new play enjoyed the same kind of business as the Brecht, and Alan Ayres's fears about its publicity proved unexpectedly groundless. Hall hoped Brenton's next venture for the National would be a translation of *Danton's Death*.

Later, Dexter's new musical was closed down during the pre-views and industrial relations trouble besieged him at the Met. In London, the board of the Royal Court extended Max Stafford-Clark's appointment as artistic director for a further three years. The National management remained formally committed to Dexter's returning there, but discussions as to what he might direct had been fitful. In October, Dexter learned from the transatlantic edition of the *Guardian* that Peter Gill – another director with a Royal Court connection – had been appointed to work alongside Hall. In November, it was announced that Dexter was to become Director of the Festival Theatre in Strat-ford, Ontario; then the Canadian government vetoed his appointment. His negotiations with the National were sub-sequently revived, and plans emerged for Dexter to direct either *The Shoemaker's Holiday* or Gambon as Coriolanus the follow-ing summer. But matching the director's availability with the National's timetable – in order to avoid precisely the kind of falling behind schedule that had bedevilled *Galileo* – proved tricky. In short, Dexter had told the actors he would see them in 1981, but the success of the Brecht production had by no means guaranteed this.

Technically, *Galileo* remained a troublesome show, and the start of one performance was delayed by a protracted change-over. A small improvement to the galaxy was brought about by moving the projectors further from the shutters. The back projectors behaved themselves in performance, but Andy Torble received an electric shock that kept him off work for several days. Although Mark Taylor had earlier said they had neither the time nor the money to replace the metal substruc-ture, the kind of wooden rostra he had wanted all along were in fact substituted in September.

By this time, with a sorry kind of inevitability, John Malone had been sacked. Stopping off at his Northumberland home between Edinburgh and London, he discovered that his wife had taken a fall and gone into labour. He opted to take some leave to see her through the birth, and in the course of this Bill Bundy phoned to break the news. The National asserted that Malone had simply not done a good enough job, and there was all-round agreement that personality conflicts had exacerbated things. But Malone believed the theatre was not as committed as it claimed to having someone do an effective job in the post he had held, and that Bundy gave more credence to what was said on the fourth floor than what was done in the workshops. Bundy promised that, in time, he would be attempting to appoint another workshops manager.

The Vatican, meanwhile, announced that it was to review its official verdict on Galileo, unchanged since the events described in Brecht's play.

And Mrs Malone's baby arrived safely.

Chapter Sixteen

Postscript

When the publishers asked the National's help with this book in principle, the theatre rapidly agreed. Muffled doubts were expressed, however, as to the wisdom of covering *Galileo* in particular. The worry was that, in the unlikely event of John Dexter's consenting to cooperate, he would throw me out before rehearsals were half complete. As it turned out, Dexter could not have been more helpful. On two occasions, for example, he changed his rehearsal plans on the spot to enable Zoë Dominic to fit in additional photographs. Whatever his methods, I certainly fell under the odd spell of his personality.

But this was only typical of the general reception we were given. Ivan Alderman made a bit of a show of being too busy to talk, though he managed to fit in an evening to tell me his life story, and he was exceedingly generous with his gin. There was a half-hearted attempt to prevent my speaking with John Malone after his dismissal. But for the most part, people were always forthcoming. The only occasion anyone refused directly to answer a question was when I asked one of the older actors his age. Even those who were at first reluctant to have their photographs taken agreed in time, for the simple reason that they felt the book could be useful to the National especially and the theatre in general.

I dwell on this because the profession usually likes to keep a bit of mystery about itself, and is singularly coy about anything touching on money. It is hard to imagine many other large arts bodies emulating the National's break with convention, but it is to be hoped that some of them will.

The National shares some faults with other institutions. There is not a single woman on its all-important panel of Associate Directors, for example. From time to time personnel are treated in a lumbering manner. To add to his woes with Dexter, Michael Fenner was twice told that he had landed a part in *The Romans in Britain* only to be told later that he had not. He was informed that the part was his a third time and there, fortunately, the matter rested. By comparison with most institutions, though, the atmosphere at the National is mercifully relaxed.

I cannot say I was surprised that money and time were spent on things for *Galileo* that were never used. Experiment – and therefore failure – are essential in artistic endeavour, and will sometimes be expensive. Waste resulted from an accumulation of unhappy accidents rather than by neglect. The fact that some of the 'changes in mind' could have been avoided does not amount to an argument against subsidy on the present or a larger scale. The National is, if anything, over-obsessed with 'public accountability'. The fracas over John Malone and the whole 22-week business were part of a continuing strategy to tighten the purse-strings. What is unfair about the National is not that it has decent resources but that other members of the theatre community – on the 'fringe' for example – do not.

In October 1974, Oscar Lewenstein and a number of other distinguished theatre people wrote to *The Times* forecasting that the National at its new home would severely drain the pool of technical labour in the rest of the profession. This fear has surely been proved unreasonable. The apprenticeships and training courses offered by the National's high-powered backstage departments increase the expertise that is generally available. What's more, they go a little way to breaking the middle-class preponderance in the theatre. Bill Bundy is keen to extend the present schemes, and the National should be encouraged to see them as a growing responsibility.

To follow the progress of *Galileo* was to realise how many misconceptions about theatre still exist. Criticism sometimes suggests that dramatic production is a linear affair, like painting – that a concept is born in an individual's mind and then executed under that individual's control. But theatre is social, and vulnerable to environment, timing, personal relationships, fashion and economics. The painter relies on paint, brushes and canvas. In theatre, individuals and groups of people rely intimately and heavily on each other, even though they may not know each other very well. Who is responsible for what is wickedly difficult to define with precision.

It was not even easy to identify the genesis of the production. Was it when Dexter saw the Berliner Ensemble in 1957? Or during a discussion between Hall and John Russell Brown in 1973? Dexter directed the show, but Brown commissioned the translation and Hall appointed the director after he had recruited the leading man. I have called what appeared in the Olivier 'John Dexter's production' as if that were a fixed entity. But suppose Peter Firth had been in the cast, as Dexter wished. The later scenes might have been more purple and the actor playing Andrea might have fared better with the critics. Equally possibly, the show might have lost some of its ascetic clarity. It would still have been 'John Dexter's production', though.

Directors are often thought to spend most of their time coaching and coaxing actors, yet Dexter was constantly referring to larger matters of *mise-en-scène*, to the logistics of his aesthetic. It is impossible to imagine the show without Jocelyn Herbert's design. The determination of Herbert and Dexter to change prevalent ideas about the Olivier was as much as anything the show's foundation.

Everything in theatre is precarious, and the dividing line between success and failure can be agonisingly fine. Knowing this, scores of very different people – including some who would never sit through a performance – threw themselves into work on *Galileo*, as they had for the show before, and would for the show after. With the exception of Howard Brenton, their commitment was professional and aesthetic rather than political or theoretical. It was also remarkably uniform.

Outsiders might be puzzled that so much went into such a fleeting event as a piece of theatre. But when Elizabeth Markham summoned the audience into the Olivier for another performance, as the tickets were torn by the National's personable front-of-house staff, when the lights dimmed, Robert Oates announced the play, the armillery sphere ascended, the choir struck up and that troublesome truck trundled Gambon forward for the start of the 'socialist classic' – then it was clear what the fuss was all about.

The 22 weeks of *Galileo*

The actual dates of rehearsals are given, and the theoretical deadlines for design, set building, etc.

Week number	Week commencing Monday	
22	3 March	Play decided
21	10 March	
20	17 March	Director, designer, lighting designer chosen
19	24 March	
18	31 March	
17	7 April	
16	14 April	Outline design presented
15	21 April	
14	28 April	Final design presented; model completed; budget settled
13	5 May	
12	12 May	Designer's drawings completed
11	19 May	
10	26 May	Work in costume dept and workshops commenced
9	2 June	
8	9 June	
7	16 June	First week of rehearsals
6	23 June	Second week of rehearsals
5	30 June	Third week of rehearsals
4	7 July	Fourth week of rehearsals
3	14 July	Fifth week of rehearsals
2	21 July	Sixth week of rehearsals ⎫ Set in rehearsal room
1	28 July	Seventh week of rehearsals ⎭
0	4 August	Production week. First preview on Friday
	11 August	Official first performance on Wednesday

The cost of *Galileo*

Originally, the National intended to spend a maximum of £45,000 on its production of *Galileo*. This was reduced to £33,000 as a result of the economic crisis. John Dexter's earliest plans would have cost £42,000 *plus* £10,000 for costumes. By the time of the production meeting, these figures had been adjusted to £38,000 and £12,000 respectively. The finally agreed budget was £33,000 plus £12,000 for costumes. As is shown below, the costumes went over by nearly £4,000 but the rest of the production was kept just within budget.

These figures include changes – such as the replacement of the disc substructure – made after the show opened; they do not include the National's internal labour costs.

Production expenditure excluding costumes

		Total £	Budget £
Scenic woodwork			
Materials bought specially	2,214.06		
Materials taken from stock	6,528.85	8,742.91	9,000
(Includes timber for the disc and truck floors, the balustrade and larger items of furniture.)			
Scenic metalwork			
Work contracted out and materials bought specially	11,239.90		
Materials taken from stock	1,728.76	12,968.66	9,500
(Includes Kemp's bill for £10,935, excluding VAT.)			
Scene painting			
Cost of materials		1,717.03	4,000
Properties			
Cost of materials and bought items		3,743.10	6,500

Production expenditure excluding costumes – *cont.*

	Total £	Budget £
Armoury	364.35	500
Electrics (Includes the printing and reprinting of slides, approximately £1,200 for the repair of condensers, and approaching £900 for cabling for the lighting rig.)	4,554.39	2,000
Production office	266.81	1,000
Sound	2.95	500
TOTALS	32,360.20	33,000

The costume bill came to £15,732.23½, including £5,052 for work contracted out and freelancers brought in specially for *Galileo*.

To estimate roughly the cost of internal labour, Bill Bundy's practice is to multiply the expenditure on materials and bought items by a maximum of 120 per cent. If this sum is done in the case of *Galileo* and the figure arrived at added to the totals above, the cost of the production remains well below £100,000. It would be unusual in this day and age for a West End musical – with which it is not altogether unfair to compare *Galileo* – to be mounted for a similarly low figure. Bill Bundy noted that *Galileo* cost less than *Amadeus*, and that its set cost roughly the same as that for *Sisterly Feelings*.

The people involved

Listed are those who both worked on *Galileo* and are mentioned in this book. People's positions are given as at the time of the production.

ALDERMAN, IVAN: the National's Costume Supervisor.

ALLEN, DAVID: member of the property workshop.

ALLEN, GAELLE: milliner (freelance).

ASHMORE, CATHERINE: assistant to photographer Zoë Dominic.

AYRES, ALAN: publicist, with particular responsibility for *Galileo*.

BARHAM, ROB: member of the armoury.

BARNARD, ROB: member of the sound department, with particular responsibility for *Galileo*.

BATA, CHARLES: member of the Olivier electrics (lighting) team.

BEAGARIE, JOYCE: Wig Mistress.

BEDFORD, MELVYN: actor playing a monk in the Collegium Romanum scene, and other parts.

BEINT, MICHAEL: actor playing Mucius and other parts including the Mathematician to the Florentine court.

BELLAIRS, NIGEL: actor playing a monk in the Collegium Romanun scene, and other parts.

BENNETT, EDMOND: actor playing the Florentine court chamberlain and other parts.

BERNARD, ROY: the Olivier's Deputy Master Carpenter; acting Master Carpenter in the absence on holiday of Dennis Nolan.

BIRTWISTLE, HARRISON: an Associate Director of the National Theatre, in charge of music.

BISSETT, ANGELA: member of the stage management team.

BOISSEAU, JAMES: member of the stage management team (prompter) who left during the rehearsal period.

BRENNER, MARC: child actor playing the younger Andrea, Giuseppe and other parts.

BRENTON, HOWARD: translator.

BROWN, JOHN RUSSELL: an Associate Director of the National Theatre, its Repertoire Adviser and head of its Script Department.

BRYCELAND, YVONNE: actress playing Mrs Sarti.

BUNDY, WILLIAM (BILL): the National's Technical Administrator.

BURROWS, STEPHEN: member of the metal workshop.

CADELL, SELINA: actress playing Virginia.

CALLOW, SIMON: actor playing Fulganzio, the Little Monk.

COLEBY, JOHN: former Rights Manager at the National.

COOPER, DONALD: photographer.

COOPER, ELLIOTT: actor playing Lodovico.

CRUICKSHANK, ANDREW: actor playing Priuli, the Bursar.

DAWSON, PETER: actor playing a monk in the Collegium Romanum scene, and other parts.

DEXTER, JOHN: director.

DIAMOND, GILLIAN: the National's Casting Director.

DIGNAM, MARK: actor playing Cardinal Bellarmin.

DOMINIC, ZOË: photographer.

DUNLOP, SUE: member of the property workshop.

DUNN, ERIC: head of the metal workshop.

ELLIOTT, MICHAEL: General Administrator of the National Theatre.

FEHR, SANDRA: actress playing the Balladeer's Wife and other parts.

FENNER, MICHAEL: actor playing the speaking Frontier Guard (before being replaced by Glenn Williams) and other parts.

GAMBON, MICHAEL: actor playing Galileo.

GARDNER, GORDON: voice coach.

GARTLAND, ROGER: actor playing the First Astronomer in the Collegium Romanum scene, and other parts.

GASH, HAZEL: member of the scenic studio (paint frame).

GOODALL, CYNTHIA: member of the costume department.

GOODFELLOW, DAVID: member of the armoury.

GOODWIN, JOHN: the National's Head of Publicity and Publications.

GREEN, RIC: Sound Manager.

HAILL, LYNN: Print Sub-Editor, Publicity and Publications department.

HALL, SIR PETER: Director of the National Theatre.

HALLIFAX, MICHAEL: the National's Company Administrator.

HARTWELL, PETER: assistant to the designer, Jocelyn Herbert.

HAYES, JAMES: actor playing Federzoni.

HENSON, BASIL: actor playing Cardinal Barberini, who becomes Pope Urban VIII.

HERBERT, JOCELYN: designer.

HOWARD, ROBERT: actor playing a philosopher in the Collegium Romanum scene, and other parts.

HULLEY, RODGER: Production Manager in the Lyttelton, acting Production Manager in the Olivier.

JESSOP, MICHAEL: member of the costume department in charge of costume accessories.

KEMP ENGINEERS LTD, P. E.: metal engineering contractors.

KENT, BRIAN: actor playing a member of the Carnival crowd and other parts including the Papal Astronomer (Christopher Clavius).

KILLIAN, ANDREW: the National's Stage Controller.

LAND, PETER: actor/singer playing the Balladeer, a Scholar in the Collegium Romanum scene, and other parts.

LEEMAN, KEVIN: the National's Music Manager; rehearsal pianist for *Galileo*.

LOMAX, HARRY: actor playing the Very Old Cardinal.

LORD, DAPHNE: maker of masks and other costume accessories (freelance) working with Michael Jessop.

MACKINTOSH, KENNETH: the National's Senior Staff Director, with particular responsibility for *Galileo*; also playing Signor Vanni.

MALONE, JOHN: the National's Workshops Manager.

MARKHAM, ELIZABETH: Deputy Stage Manager.

MARSHALL, PEGGY: actress playing the Lady in Waiting at the Florentine court, and other parts.

MAYER, CASSANDRA: member of the Publicity and Publications department, with particular responsibility for press tickets.

MIDDLETON, MICHELLE: child actress playing the Balladeer's daughter.

MOGFORD, JOHN: employee of P. E. Kemp Engineers Ltd.

MOORE, STEPHEN: actor playing the Cardinal Inquisitor.

MORRIS, ARTRO: actor playing the Fat Prelate in the Collegium Romanum scene, and other parts.

MULDOWNEY, DOMINIC: Music Director of the National Theatre, and for *Galileo*.

NEEDHAM, PETER: actor playing the Second Astronomer in the Collegium Romanum scene, and other parts.

NOLAN, DENNIS: the Olivier's Master Carpenter.

NORTON, ADAM: actor playing the Thin Monk in the Collegium Romanum scene, and other parts.

NORTON, TIMOTHY: child actor playing Prince Cosimo de Medici and other parts.

OATES, ROBERT: actor playing The Speaker.

PHILLIPS, ANDY: lighting designer.

PHILLIPS, JOHN: the National's Head of Scenic Construction (carpenters' workshop).

POCOCK, RICHARD: member of the property workshop.

PRICE, AUDREY: costumier (freelance).

PURSEY, JOHNNY: head of the (stage) property department.

RADMORE, PETER: Chief Electrician in the Olivier.

RASSOU, YVES: Head of the National's Scenic Studio (paint frame).

ROBINSON, ANN: Casting Assistant.

ROONEY, STEPHEN: child actor appearing in the 'Pope dressing' and other scenes.

ROTHENBERG, JOHN: Stage Manager.

SALTMAN, BARRY: the National's Armourer.

SKAPTASON, STEPHEN: Chief Cutter in the costume department.

STAFFORD, ADAM: child actor playing the First Boy in the final (frontier) scene, and other parts.

STALKER-CLARKE, LEE: member of the metal workshop.

STANFORD, JILL: actress playing the Younger Lady in Waiting at the Florentine court, and other parts.

STARSHINE, SYLVIA: member of the metal workshop.

SUTTON, ALAN: carpenter; son and partner to Doug Sutton.

SUTTON, DOUG: carpenter; father and partner to Alan Sutton.

TAYLOR, MARK: Assistant Production Manager in the Olivier.

THOMAS, LENNIE: Head Flyman.

THOMAS, MICHAEL: actor playing the older Andrea.

THORNDIKE, DANIEL: actor playing the Philosopher to the Florentine court, and other parts.

TORBLE, ANDY: member of the Olivier electrics (lighting) team.

WARE, NEVILLE: member of the stage management team who joined during the rehearsal period and replaced James Boisseau.

WELCH, PETER: actor recruited during the rehearsal period to understudy the part of Galileo.

WHITING, GORDON: actor playing the Theologian to the Florentine court, and other parts.

WILLIAMS, GLENN: actor playing a Scholar in the Collegium Romanum scene, the speaking Frontier Guard (after replacing Michael Fenner) and other parts.